MW00584474

GAMING
AND THE
HEROIC LIFE

"This book is both timely and relevant as we seek to reach the next generation. *Gaming and the Heroic Life* continues the work of the New Evangelization by branching into a topic not much discussed but very much needed in the Church. As is evidenced by the recent beatification of Blessed Carlos Acutis, video game culture will be a pivotal place of catechesis and encounter in the years to come, and this book will prove a valuable tool to that end."

Fr. Blake Britton
Author of *Reclaiming Vatican II*

"I'm not a gamer myself. My experience of video games mostly consisted of sitting in the chair next to my older siblings watching as *they* played games. But Bobby Angel has translated the ways in which video games can foster virtue for even a rookie like me. Bobby's insight into the world of video games, young people, and the life of virtue has qualified him in a unique way to offer the wisest counsel for anyone interested in all three."

Fr. Mike Schmitz
Host of *The Bible in a Year* podcast

"As a mother who also has a ministry to young adults, I am so grateful to Bobby Angel for writing this book! It is full of faithful insight, keen direction, and answers to challenging questions! *Gaming and the Heroic Life* is a must read for gamers seeking to take their own gaming experience (and life) to a deeper level, and a must read for non-gamers seeking to understand the appeal and fulfillment that comes from gaming. This book has been a gift to me, and I know it will be a gift to many!"

Sarah Swafford
Catholic speaker and author of *Emotional Virtue*

"With the soul of a gamer and a heart for Jesus, Bobby really nails the mission field of gaming that a lot of people simply overlook. This is a perfect guide to being in the culture but not of it. It's dangerous to go alone—take this book!"

Katie Ruvalcaba
Twitch streamer @MrsRuvi

GAMING
AND THE
HEROIC LIFE

A QUEST FOR HOLINESS IN
THE VIRTUAL WORLD

BOBBY ANGEL

AVE MARIA PRESS AVE Notre Dame, Indiana

Scripture quotations are from *Revised Standard Version of the Bible*, copyright ©
1946, 1952, and 1971 National Council of the Churches of Christ in the United
States of America. Used by permission. All rights reserved worldwide.

Passages marked *CCC* are from the English translation of the *Catechism
of the Catholic Church* for the United States of America, copyright
1994, United States Catholic Conference, Inc.—Libreria Editrice Vaticana.
Used with permission.

Foreword © 2023 by Jonathan "Bearded" Blevins

© 2023 by Robert Angel

All rights reserved. No part of this book may be used or reproduced in any manner whatsoever, except in the case of reprints in the context of reviews, without
written permission from Ave Maria Press®, Inc., P.O. Box 428, Notre Dame, IN
46556, 1-800-282-1865.

Founded in 1865, Ave Maria Press is a ministry of the United States Province of
Holy Cross.

www.avemariapress.com

Paperback: ISBN-13 978-1-64680-249-4

E-book: ISBN-13 978-1-64680-250-0

Cover images © AdobeStock.

Cover and text design by Christopher D. Tobin.

Printed and bound in the United States of America.

Library of Congress Cataloging-in-Publication Data is available.

For all the young (and not so young) gamers out there:
God sees you and loves you
and desires your best life possible.

CONTENTS

FOREWORD

"Can you be Christian and play video games?"

As someone who streams video games in front of tens of thousands of people every day, I know gamers are wondering about this question because it comes up in our exchanges all the time. Our world needs this book. Finally, we have a gamer and missionary disciple leading the conversation about video games and their impact on the human person.

I grew up in a gaming household. Both of my brothers are still avid gamers—one teaches high school students and plays games in his free time; the other just happens to be the most well-known video gamer in the world, Tyler "Ninja" Blevins. Sharing video games as we grew up created amazing memories—stories we still talk about today.

Our parents did a great job of making sure we lived a balanced life. My brothers and I played three sports each all year long and did fairly well in school. To balance those commitments, we were allowed to play video games for only a few hours on the weekends. Even though our video game time was limited, some of my favorite memories from my childhood come from gaming with my brothers.

We love playing *Pokémon*, for example; when we were allowed to bring our Gameboys on long road trips to grandma and grandpa's house, we could communicate without fighting for hours on end. We would also make forts in our room and stay up playing with our Gameboy lights clipped to the top of our devices, laughing late into the night. I don't remember anything that happened on those Gameboys, but I do remember the laughter and the joy.

I think many people have experiences like this—so many friendships are forged through video gaming together. As kids, once every few months we would link our Xboxes downstairs for a "LAN party" and have friends over to play *Halo*. Again, I don't remember much about the game itself, but I will never forget the camaraderie that came with playing it together.

I played *Halo 2* with my brother, Tyler, for years. When I was nineteen, *Halo 3* dropped and we were so excited. I waited in line at midnight to get the game, but Tyler was only sixteen—our parents wouldn't let him stay up to play because it was a school night. He was so disappointed. I got home around one in the morning and decided to wake him up to play for an hour as a surprise. To this day, he talks about how this was one of the coolest moments of his life. We played a few duo games, won them all, and then when the weekend hit, that's all we did. I have since apologized to my parents for keeping Tyler up that night, but looking back, they love that I created that moment with my brother.

I communicate with gamers for a living and feel lucky to interact with an amazing community. I know what gamers are struggling with and what they are curious about. In the conversations that unfold on my streaming platforms, I hear the same questions people have been asking for a long time: who am I, and what is my purpose? This book tackles these questions head-on and invites you to reflect on the places you look for answers. This book also surfaces a lot of questions you maybe didn't even know you were asking.

Video games are not evil, but they also shouldn't have a negative impact on our lives. How do we find that balance? How do we navigate these new waters? Can we live God's call for our lives and have video games play a major role in them? Can I have a consistent prayer life and enjoy gaming?

This book answers many of these questions and then some. I don't just wish that I could have read this book when I was in high school or college—I wish I could have given it to my parents as well. I did not have the words to describe why I liked video games so much, but I knew that it wasn't simply because they were fun. I knew the kinds of experiences I was having in a game—confronting challenges, building teamwork, developing skills, taking bold action, and savoring beautiful images and music—were resonating on a deep level. In a way, these experiences were helping me develop a desire for greatness, a desire that has led me to a deeper relationship with God.

The stories we join when playing video games give us glimpses of the true, the good, and the beautiful. Bobby reveals how whenever and wherever we encounter these values, we experience transcendence—our minds and hearts are lifted upward. As long as they don't become ends in themselves, video games can inspire us to search for something more in our lives. If our real lives pale in comparison to defeating villains, accomplishing missions, and earning victories on a screen, we're missing out on a life of adventure with God.

Being a Christian doesn't mean running away from the world. It means having the courage and faith to plunge deeper into it. Because God is so radically committed to us, there is no place where we can't find him—including video games. This book equips gamers with an understanding of why we love video games—and how they can help us become who we were created to be.

So can you be Christian and play video games? Not only is it possible to enjoy video games and be madly in love with God, but also—as Bobby shows here—with the right approach, video games can actually inspire you to strive for the greatness to which God is calling you.

Jonathan "Bearded" Blevins
CEO of Little Flower Media

INTRODUCTION

I was about seven years old when I fell in love with video games. My uncle Bob allowed my younger brother and me to "borrow" his Super Nintendo. We never gave it back.

My *earliest* memory of a video game was *Duck Hunt* on the original Nintendo. You had to aim a plastic gun clunkily at the TV screen and were subjected to an obnoxious dog's laughter every time you missed a shot. Alongside the *Pac-Man* and *Space Invaders* offerings at the local arcade, this was the burgeoning era of console games in all their eight-bit glory.

But it was interacting with the second generation of gaming consoles—namely, the Super Nintendo and the Sega Genesis—that changed my life. Games weren't solely about button-mashing or puzzled blocks falling from the sky anymore—games were now offering narratives that moved me, heroes who inspired me, and music that burrowed into my ears. Video games were becoming an interactive art form, and instead of watching a movie or reading a book about a protagonist, I could *become* the protagonist. I could travel around that imaginary world and fight the battles that needed fighting and make a difference in a way that only I could. And unless the games were needlessly difficult or poorly constructed, they were absolutely *fun*.

From blue-shelling my family members in *Mario Kart* and sniping friends in *GoldenEye* to LAN (local area network) *Halo* tournaments, games also brought me together with people from all walks of life: from classmates to neighbors, dorm buddies, and beyond. I loved (and still love) solitary gameplay, but I have also witnessed how video games can bring people together—both locally and even from around the world.

As a gangly young man, thoroughly uncoordinated in all manners of catching or throwing a ball, I additionally found that I didn't have to prove myself to my peers in the arena of video games. Here was a field where your athletic prowess (or lack thereof) didn't matter. My own physical insecurities, stemming from a total lack of competency in "normal ball sports," gave way once I found the fields in which I could compete well, such as swimming, track, and other endurance sports. But video games remained an emotional and mental refuge after a long day.

As my time in high school began to come to a close (and video games continued to mature in their storytelling), I found myself also wrestling with deeper questions. Video games had rapidly changed from mindless entertainment to something that gave me great stories and worlds to explore. But in the nonvirtual world, how would my life pan out? What was *my* hero's journey? Who would be part of my tribe or clan once high school ended? Did I have a great adventure before me?

I was excellent in the virtual world . . . but how could I be excellent in the real world?

I also found myself questioning my Catholic Christian faith. I grew up in the Church—altar serving, giving to the poor, and helping out at the occasional bingo night—but I wouldn't describe my faith as something rooted in a living, breathing reality of God's love. Jesus was a *part* of my life, but certainly not at the center of my life. I thought that being Catholic was a nice, moral way to live life but not a "really real" thing. I knew *about* Jesus, but I didn't *know* Jesus.

Video games seemed to answer the cry of my heart—that longing for adventure and meaning—more than the Christian faith did. I couldn't wait to get back to my PlayStation once church was over. I remember daydreaming my way during most Masses, imagining, for instance, that ninjas or dragons would come crashing through the stained-glass windows—epic battles would, of course, then ensue. I had to snap out of these visions while altar serving on more than one occasion, embarrassed that the priest was waiting on me to bring him the holy vessels because I was caught up in defending the church from imaginary ninjas.

Then in my senior year of high school, I experienced God's love in a profound "really real" way. After getting involved in a youth group with dynamic leaders and peers, experiencing Eucharistic Adoration and my first summer youth conference, and benefiting from serious prayer from friends and mentors, my heart was ready to see the God who was waiting on me from all eternity. I fell in love with the Lord, and a new, strange, and exciting chapter of my life opened up.

I asked tough questions of my faith and grew in knowledge and conviction. I started to ask questions of my beloved video games too, which I still played throughout college. I'm still asking these questions as a husband and father.

When it comes to both video games and my faith, all of my searching can be boiled down to two questions:

Lord, how can I best love and serve you today?

and

Am I living a good life?

Sometimes we don't think that video games and the Christian faith are compatible. We have examples of faith and sports coming together with many athletes wearing their faith on their sleeves, but not so much in the world of video games. Our wider culture can still offer a remnant of belittling attitudes toward people who play video games, disregarding the medium as purely mindless entertainment that dooms individuals to live in the basements of their parents.

Sometimes we hear that games are responsible for every tragic mass shooting, or they are demonized entirely wholesale (I've actually heard someone say, "*Super Mario* is just as bad as *Grand Theft Auto*"). For people of faith, many assume that our spiritual life has zero bearing on what we play at all (and vice versa), so these concerns seem silly, outdated, and not worth entertaining; in fact, to game at all seems like an irrelevant matter in life.

That's why I wrote this book: to meet these questions head-on and demonstrate that we can love gaming and love God at the same time—in fact, we can love God *through* our gaming.

What I have found beautiful about being a follower of Christ is that Jesus does not repress our humanity or make us into mindless, holy clones. The saints were the men and women throughout history who were the most unique and most passionately on fire with divine love. They understood the adventure of being known and loved and sent out on a mission by God, and this love transformed their relationships, their occupations, and even their hobbies.

Living a good life—a life of excellence and virtue—has Christ as its center, above all else. This does not mean we lose who we are and what we love doing—whether art, athletics, hobbies, or even video games. It simply means that our identity becomes rooted so much deeper in the reality of God's love and that our own lives are transformed to give glory to God and new life to others. Because God is so near to us, we don't have to let go of the interests that capture our hearts. The goodness we experience in those interests shares in God's goodness. Being a person of faith doesn't mean I have to turn away from the things of this world. They can actually point me to God if I keep them rightly ordered and don't approach them as the most important thing in my life.

When Benedict XVI was elected pope, his first message included these words: "Do not be afraid of Christ! He takes nothing away, and he gives you everything. When we give ourselves to him, we receive a hundredfold in return."[1] In the pages that follow, I hope to convince you of this good news.

Game on, my friends!

Bobby Angel
Penned on October 12, 2022, the Feast of Bl. Carlo Acutis

LEVEL 1

1

WHY WE LOVE GAMES

Whenever I hear from someone, "Well, I don't play games . . . ," my response is always the same: "*Everybody* games!"

The ancient Egyptians played a game called *senet*, and the Chinese played mah-jongg; pottery from antiquity shows Achilles and Ajax playing on a board with dice, and the "Royal Game of Ur" dates to some four thousand years ago in ancient Mesopotamia.

"The Games" of Rome featured chariot races and gladiatorial matches to entertain thousands, and the Olympic games of ancient Greece evolved from a locals-only show of strength to a universal competition in which athletes from all nations could participate. From crossword puzzles and chess to soccer tournaments and sumo wrestling, from fencing to Formula One to four square, and from sudoku to the Super Bowl, there seems to be this common bond across all of humanity: *Everybody* games!

Let's jump to the introduction of electricity and the leaps in technology since the nineteenth century, culminating in radios, television, the internet, and smartphones. Game shows like *Wheel of Fortune*, *Jeopardy*, and singing competitions continue to dominate the airwaves. The first video game predated 1972's *Pong* by more than a decade when nuclear physicist William Higinbotham created *Tennis for Two* in 1958, which used an analog vacuum-tube computer to depict a blurry little dot being lobbed over a net on a five-inch screen.

Today, entire *arenas* are being constructed not for gladiatorial death matches but for spectators to watch video gamers destroy one another's pixelated avatars. The video game industry's revenue came in at around $155 billion in 2020. And 75 percent of Americans have at least one gaming device in their homes, be it a personal computer (PC), a console (Nintendo, PlayStation, or Xbox), or the smartphone in their pockets.

From *Candy Crush* to *Super Mario Bros.*, and from *Fortnite* to FIFA, *everybody* games!

A (SHORT) HISTORY OF VIDEO GAMES

To adequately cover the meteoric rise of the video game industry would require a book unto itself. Many articles, blogs, and documentaries already exist that record the emergence and evolution of video games. We will paint with some broad strokes for the sake of an overview here before moving on to why it matters that we've always played games.

We can trace the beginnings of modern video games to the nuclear physicist William Higinbotham and his creation of *Tennis for Two*. Up to this point, video games were dots and blips on wall-sized machines housed in universities and labs like MIT during the days of the Cold War. Later, the 1970s and '80s gave rise to the popularity of classics like 1978's *Space Invaders*, and then *Pac-Man* took hold of a generation. (Fun fact: The ever-increasing speed of *Space Invaders* was unintended; the game developer had trouble programming a consistent speed so it was kept in the game, leading to an inevitably addictive challenge.) Arcades became popular sites among the young as these "video games" started to rival the pool tables and pinball machines for attention.

In 1975, Atari became the first truly "home console" system that brought the play of the arcade home in a real and effective way; *Pong* was the most recognized game in its library. From there, the gaming industry blossomed—but almost crashed completely in the mid-1980s due to an oversaturation of subpar consoles, sloppily churned-out, poor-quality games, and competition from newly affordable home computers. The industry was saved when Nintendo introduced the Nintendo Entertainment System (NES) in 1985 and poured resources into ensuring that their games were tested and of high quality. The company Sega wasn't far behind, and the two Japanese companies successfully rescued what could have been the very short-lived phenomenon of home video game consoles.

Before long, characters such as Super Mario, Zelda, Donkey Kong, and Sonic the Hedgehog became just as recognizable as Mickey Mouse and were now part of pop culture itself. Handheld devices such as Nintendo's Gameboy or Sega's Game Gear also took off in popularity—now kids could play video games on the go! Going after older gamers and tackling more mature subjects, Sony's PlayStation system debuted in 1993, and Microsoft's Xbox was released in 2001, both featuring robust libraries of games; both companies still dominate in gaming sales to this day. PC gaming also steadily rose to prominence and continues to attract a loyal fanbase. As the technology advanced from eight bit to sixteen bit and then to thirty-two bit, the mode of play also changed from hard gaming cartridges to CDs that featured greater storage space. (Fun fact: As of writing, we're currently in the 1,024-bit generation with the PlayStation 5, Nintendo Switch, and Xbox Series X).

While single-player games remain popular, gaming has never been a solitary endeavor. As communal creatures, we enjoy getting to play with and against other people. Being able to play with someone else once meant sitting with a sibling or friend on the living room floor with a wired controller. The Nintendo 64 debuted in 1996 and featured the innovative ability for four people to play together at the same time. Microsoft's Xbox then raised the stakes by allowing multiple consoles to be physically linked together through local area network (LAN) cables. Consoles and PCs could be connected so that eight (or more!) people could play together in the same physical space, and "LAN parties" became serious business for gamers throughout the early 2000s.

Around the same time, there was also a strange new game called *Pokémon* that arrived on the shores of America. The yellow Pikachu character was suddenly on a cartoon show and being merchandised on every lunchbox and plush toy. The thought-to-be-dead Gameboy was suddenly *the* console every kid needed in order to play the original *Pokémon*. Video games were now changing culture itself at a broad level, and the *Pokémon* phenomenon demonstrated the far-reaching power of the industry.

High-speed internet and Wi-Fi changed the landscape of gaming once again. Home consoles could now connect to the internet for faster play, and more players could be engaged at the same time (the popular battle royale game *Fortnite*, for example, features one-hundred players in a last-man-standing format). Games can now be downloaded straight to the hard drive of the system (no more CDs or cartridges needed), and players can even purchase weapons, costumes, powers, and so forth with real money ("microtransactions") for added advantages in gameplay.

Mobile phone gaming is also a force unto itself. The first iPhone debuted in 2007, and Apple's *Texas Hold'em* poker game was released as the first game in their App Store. "Smartphones" quickly went beyond texts, maps, and messaging as developers created applications (apps) of games by the thousands. Millions of people were sucked into the worlds of *Angry Birds*, *Candy Crush*, *Temple Run*, *Clash of Clans*, *FarmVille*, and all their variations. Games account for 43 percent of all smartphone use; the number of active mobile gamers worldwide is estimated at more than two billion.[1]

According to a report from the Digital Entertainment and Retail Association, gaming is the largest home entertainment sector in the UK, having earned around £4.66 billion (around $5.66 billion) in revenue in 2022.[2] Gaming arenas continue to be constructed, and e-sports leagues and tournaments rise in popularity and recognition against traditional physical sports. Video games increasingly shape pop culture, with Illumination Studio's 2023 film *Super Mario Bros.* scoring the top all-time opening weekend for an animated film with $375.6 million in worldwide ticket sales. Virtual reality (VR) and augmented reality technologies are being developed to further merge the space between physical and digital existence. Developers continue to push the limits of systems' graphics, speed, and connectivity beyond what we could have imagined decades ago.

Video gaming is here to stay!

WHY GAME AT ALL?

Pardon the philosophical detour within the first chapter here, but we need to face an important question that few people ever ask and one that's vital to where this book is headed: *why* do we game in the first place?

Playing games, whether athletic, tabletop, or digital, is an amazing phenomenon, to be sure. We don't *need* to play games to exist as a species. After food, water, and shelter, gameplay *still* doesn't rank among the top necessities for survival. But the same could be said about art, music, romance, or even friendship. We don't *need* these phenomena to live, but it wouldn't be a life much worth living without them.

A fantastic passage from C. S. Lewis's *The Four Loves* sums up this reality: "Friendship is unnecessary, like philosophy, like art, like the universe itself (for God did not need to create). It has no survival value; rather it is one of those things which give value to survival."[3]

Games are likewise "unnecessary." But so much of what makes life rich and wonderful is exactly that which is "unnecessary" and "un-useful." For instance, I love movie soundtracks. I always have an epic musical score on, whether I'm exercising, writing a blog (or this book), or even brushing my teeth ("Do you really need the *Gladiator* soundtrack on while you floss?" my wife asks me. "Yes, honey—yes, I do."). I *could* live without music, but what an impoverished life that would be!

Some of my favorite memories in life involve the game *Super Mario Kart*. The game has gone through many variations on several systems, but I can recall flying around the sixteen-bit corners on the Super Nintendo, blue-shelling my brother constantly and going for the "big jump" on Rainbow Road, and playing deliriously late into the night with college dormmates. As an absolutely unessential activity, *Mario Kart* has been an essentially enriching activity for my life and friendships, and I can bet that you have games—virtual or physical—that have brought great joy to your life as well.

PLAY!

So games serve *some* kind of purpose for a fully human life. OK, but *why*? In 1938, Dutch historian and cultural theorist Johan Huizinga dedicated an entire book to the philosophy of gameplay: *Homo Ludens* (literally, "humans playing"). Indeed, Huizinga writes, games serve the purpose of releasing energy and aggression, teaching us life lessons (especially through cooperation within sports teams), and creating and fostering social bonds. But there's something *more* to our human need to play that goes beyond mere biological usefulness: "The fun of playing resists all analysis, all logical interpretation . . . it

is precisely this fun-element that characterizes the essence of play. .
. . The very existence of play continually confirms the supra-logical
nature of the human situation. Animals play, so they must be more
than merely mechanical things. We play and know that we play, so
we must be more than merely rational beings, for play is irrational."[4]
  It's this irrationality of gameplay that is key to the fun of it all. It
is in the *act* of playing that we somehow become more human. Play
doesn't need to serve a useful purpose, although there might be con-
structive effects that come from it (and there are indeed many). But
we don't play for the sake of the side effects. If you brought a baseball
team together for the sole purpose of learning better teamwork, you
would lose the fun of the game. Life lessons and overall well-being
are side effects, not the central point, Huizinga argues.
  The point of play *is* the play.
  As with most aspects of life, this nugget is frustratingly simple
yet exceedingly profound.

THE IMPORTANCE OF LEISURE

At some point in life, we lose the joy of play for its own sake. "Unpro-
ductive" hobbies fall by the wayside, and play is demonized as "a
waste of time." We grow up and are told that the games must end.
  In the modern world, we have an unhealthy preoccupation with
productivity, a culture of endless hustle and life hacks so we can
optimize everything in our lives. We are obsessed with metrics and
tallying our screen time, to the point where we think rest is the
enemy. The majority of Americans do not use up the vacation days
and paid time off they accrue from their employers.[5] This could
be due to a host of factors: the cost or inconvenience of traveling,
the guilt of taking time away from our work, or a "savior complex"
that assumes the world will collapse if we drop off the grid. I think
a deeper root is the compulsion of our need to always be busy. We
have lost the enjoyment of simple play.
  Another key factor in this cultural workaholism, I would argue,
is a fear of silence and an inability to enter into a posture of authentic
rest. Leisure, properly understood, is not passive laziness, as when I
endlessly scroll on my phone or allow the fifth episode of the sitcom
to start autoplaying, but the ability to be renewed and restored. I

don't think it is a coincidence, for example, that the root of the word *recreation* is to be "re-created." This happens through activities that are part of a full human experience: art and music, exercise and time in nature, conversation with friends about things that truly matter, and yes, even play. Games are truly the most "useless" of activities, but they fill us up for a reason. Leisure reminds us why life matters.

Leisure is not something we "put up with" to recharge our batteries in order to get back to working. The philosopher Aristotle affirmed this more than two thousand years ago when he wrote, "We are unleisurely in order to have leisure." Read that pithy line again. Most of us believe the inverse of it.

Many of us think that life is about climbing career ladders, reaching milestones, and warding off boredom at every turn. The deeper questions of life then are shoved far down into our subconscious, but they always return, especially those nagging questions, "Who am I?" and "What am I made for?" As we'll see later, video games often aren't distracting us from those questions, but they do seem to be the only cultural voices *answering* them.

Authentic play and leisure fill up our tank and remind us that we are made for more than diplomas, degrees, and endless work. Play is *healing* and essential to our well-being. At its best, play can free our creativity and reminds us of the joy for which we have been created.

WHY GAMES MATTER

Of course, play can also be overdone or worshipped as an end in itself. Video games and professional sports alike can both occupy an inordinate amount of our time and attention (this will be examined deeper in a later chapter). Suffice it to say, for now, we all know individuals (and it might even be true of ourselves) who give the highest attention and energy to games of some kind. But that's because games *are* indeed important.

Play is meaningful. That is, games can have deep meaning that goes beyond the surface level of the gameplay. The Super Bowl is a football game, but it's not *just* a game—not for the players or the fans (and certainly not for the advertisers). Neither is that late-night death match of *Halo* with your closest friends "just a game." Michael Jordan's final career basket, a game-winning shot that clinched the 1998 NBA title, was a moment filled with meaning, just as was the last tabletop game of Scrabble with your grandmother who fought to the end. Deep meaning is ascribed to the time and energy that we invest in gameplay, whether real or virtual, and just because an activity might not have productive value doesn't mean the game is void of meaning.

Consider the unique way that games are structured and their relationship to meaning. In her book *Reality Is Broken: Why Games Make Us Better and How They Can Change the World*, game designer and author Jane McGonigal notes that across the many genres and varieties of games, there are four commonalities to their structure. Each game has (1) a goal, (2) rules, (3) a feedback system, and (4) voluntary participation. A quick survey of her points will be valuable for our later discussion within this book.

The goal of a game is the sense of purpose—what's the *point* that directs our effort? Are you keeping your virtual farm alive, moving the ball down the field, or piecing together the *Tetris* blocks chaotically falling from the sky? If the goal is unclear or muddled, we won't play the game. American spectators often view games like cricket or rugby with confusion because the point of the play, and its unique rules, don't yet make sense.

Of course, every game has *rules*. From the earliest ages, children create games of their own imagination, from the kitchen floor to the playground, and there are *always* rules to the game, even if they're made up on the spot: "You can't do that!" "That's not fair!" "He's cheating!" To play a game without rules means that the game inevitably breaks down when players end up frustrated and quit.

Ironically, the limitations of the rules actually unleash our creativity and foster strategic thinking: "By removing or limiting the obvious ways of getting to the goal, the rules push players to explore previously uncharted possibility spaces," McGonigal writes.[6] Like respecting the rules of music theory, a pianist is more creative when they know the rules of the piano and discipline their skills, instead of banging away on the keys and calling the chaos it produces "music." When we find the constraints of the map or the weapons in the video game, we have to adapt and think creatively to solve the problem before us.

The game's feedback system is also important because, without clarifying information, we have no idea whether our performance is up to snuff. A teacher who doesn't give out grades might seem like a wonderful idea if you're the student, but then you realize that you have no idea whether you're on the right track to mastering the subject matter. A boss who never gives a performance review is ultimately failing to encourage and build up his or her staff. "Real-time feedback serves as a promise to the players that the goal is definitely achievable, and it provides motivation to keep playing."[7] In games, this is shown in scoring points, gaining experience, unlocking new levels, and approaching a clear outcome of when the game ends.

Lastly, you have to be free to play the game. Games that are coerced are no fun for the player or the other participants. Everyone's miserable when only one person actually enjoys Monopoly at the dinner table. There's an understandable recoil when the player is forced against his or her will into unfair circumstances or a ghastly event (such as in dystopian fiction and films like *The Hunger Games* or *Squid Game*). Voluntary participation means that the game remains fun—that we play willingly and freely.

Graphics, storylines, difficulty-increasing algorithms, and online play are all secondary elements to these four crucial components of gameplay. Even "winning" is not the defining feature of great gameplay. McGonigal cites the philosopher Bernard Suits's definition of a game to sum up the sheer fun and irrationality of our delight in games: "Playing a game is the voluntary attempt to overcome unnecessary obstacles."[8]

LET'S JUST PLAY ALREADY!

At some point, we grow impatient in hearing all the rules, and we just want to play the game—"I'll figure it out as I go!" As in games, so in life. Experience and living life are often where we learn the best life lessons.

The first time my brother and I played Nintendo's *Super Smash Bros.*, for instance, it was utter chaos—beautiful, beautiful chaos. The game (now a franchise with several entries) throws together beloved video game characters, and you simply fight each other until the last player standing wins. Several people can play at once with items and explosives constantly falling from the sky. It's sheer madness, until you figure out *how* to make sense of the controls. When you learn the point and rules of the game, then the fun finally begins. Lots of laughter has ensued over the years as I've played (and lost) many, many rounds of *Smash Bros.* with friends of all stripes and ages.

As we examined earlier, games are indeed totally unnecessary for living, but games enrich our lives and somehow make us more human (and everyone games, whether they admit it or not!). Games can bring about deep human connections and refresh us as authentic forms of leisure. But as we know, there are also important additional factors that form us as human beings, and games often echo those greater realities.

Let's zoom out now to a few higher-level questions that we'll explore ahead:

- Games have rules, but where do our rules and sense of morality even come from? How do we define something as "good" or "bad"?

- Games are beautiful, but what makes something beautiful? Where does beauty come from?

- Games are created realities, but what (or who) created our reality? How did this all begin?

Let's continue seeking and searching, for the answers await us ahead!

QUESTIONS FOR REFLECTION

- What is the first game you ever played?

- What game has made the greatest impact in your life?

- What are your favorite forms of leisure? What "fills up your tank"?

- Apply Jane McGonigal's four factors of a good game (a clear goal, defined rules, a feedback system, and voluntary participation) to your favorite game.

- Do you agree with the statement that games are unnecessary, but also necessary?

2

WHAT IS THE GOOD LIFE?

The TV at the gym switched from its usual programming to a commercial that featured soldiers clashing with robots, explosions and car chases, and a fire-breathing dragon that swooped overhead. None of it made any sense, but it was absolutely delightful, and I felt like I was back altar serving and daydreaming of fighting the ninjas that crashed through the stained-glass windows. It seemed as if someone found my imagination and turned it into a fully funded Michael Bay movie. I then noticed a few famous characters from some video game franchises fighting in the background and realized, *Wait, this is a video game commercial.*[1]

The narrator of the commercial wrapped up his monologue of inspirational slogans as he himself leaped into the fray, and I took off my headphones to hear his last words: "Who are you to deny greatness? If you would deny it to yourself, you would deny it to the entire world!" Then, as the camera rises above the chaos of the battlefield, the tagline comes across the screen: GREATNESS AWAITS, followed by the PlayStation game company logo.

I almost applauded, right there in the middle of the gym (but I didn't). I remember thinking, *Yes . . . that is what we all desire.* Gaming companies and developers get it: we are not happy or satisfied with a mediocre life. We aren't meant simply to jump through career hoops, check the boxes society tells us to, and then retire and die. We are built for adventure, challenge, and purpose. We desire the beautiful and long for the ability to make a difference with our limited time here on earth.

Even though the commercial was calling us to virtual magnif-
icence, its message to the human heart was compelling and clear:
You are meant for greatness.

NOT MEANT FOR COMFORT

There is a fantastic quote that is often attributed to Pope Benedict
XVI: "The world offers you comfort, but you were not made for
comfort. You were made for greatness!" The only problem is that
the pope never said this—not directly at least. The pope's words
and phrases were often lost in translation or twisted by newspapers,
which is nothing new. Sadly, you can't trust everything you read in
internet memes.

But Pope Benedict *did* write an echo of this message in his papal
document *Spe Salvi (On Christian Hope)*. "Man was created for
greatness—for God himself; he was created to be filled by God," the
pope wrote, "but his heart is too small for the greatness to which it
is destined. It must be stretched. . . . This requires hard work and is
painful, but in this way alone do we become suited to that for which
we are destined" (33).

We know at some deep, interior level we are called beyond
mediocrity. A life of "just phoning it in" does not satisfy the deepest
reaches of our hearts. The beautiful reality is that God himself has
planted this call to be great within us. The problem is that we settle
our sights on things that will never fully satisfy us or lead to our
flourishing. Frustrated, we usually fall back into cyclical habits and
vices to numb ourselves and simply cope with discomfort or the
dissatisfaction of life.

"Our Lord finds our desires not too strong, but too weak," noted
C. S. Lewis.[2] We all too easily settle for the quick fix of mediocrity
instead of pursuing the banquet feast of excellence. Or as bishop and
preacher Fulton Sheen wrote, "Mediocrity is a sin against ourselves,
a kind of sacrilege. The *ennui* some hearts feel is nothing but the
instinctive reaction of their great and underdeveloped possibilities
in the face of the triviality and mediocrity of their lives."[3]

We're called to more than just the boredom of routine and the
drama of dysfunctional relationships that we see on reality TV. We
need to be shaken awake, for God wants to shatter what we have

come to accept as mind-numbingly "normal." The Spirit always beckons us to open our eyes to the possibilities of life.

Jason Craig, author and cofounder of Fraternus, an organization for forming young men, writes, "It's a bit of a paradox—we were made to be filled to the brim with something we are incapable of being filled with. But this is why he says your heart must be stretched. They must be stretched because they have been restricted by our self-absorption . . . [greatness] is born from a life submitted to God, and [our hearts are] stretched so as to have an even greater capacity for love."[4]

Pope Benedict and so many leaders of the Church assure us that greatness and the heroic life can never be found in fleeting things—popularity, pleasure, power, or wealth—but only in God himself. When we honor God first, then everything else in life falls into its right place. Only then can we start living joyfully and discover the greatness we seek.

So if we're aiming at becoming heroic men and women, we must first reframe our image of a "good life" and open up to something explosively grander than we've imagined for ourselves. Let's break down this concept of what we mean by "the good life" and how pursuing this intentionally can lead to our greatness.

THE GOOD LIFE

If you're going to win a battle royale match or school your friend in a race, it's quite essential to know the map you're playing on and where you're actually going. Without knowing your directions, you will be flailing about and likely lose the match. Likewise, in the challenge of being a human person here on earth, we need to know *where* we're going if we're going to live life well.

Aristotle compares the human person to two archers. One knows where the target is, while the other does not. Obviously, the first archer has a much better shot at hitting his mark, whereas the second *might* hit the board but only out of luck (and the second archer will likely hurt themself or others in their fumbling). We are too often like the second archer, notes Aristotle, for we all desire a good life but we don't know what that really is. We need to become clear on the right goal and how to get there.

So what is a good life, then, and how do we get there?

First of all, if we're going to ask what a good life is for a human person, it helps to know *what* we are. The nature of a thing (a hammer or a chair, for instance) dictates what its purpose is. For instance, a chair, a dolphin, or a houseplant all look like something quite different than that of a human being. Of course, we can use something *against* its nature (using a hammer for a chair or using a chair like a hammer) and thus experience the consequences, but such action never invalidates the fact that everything does have a nature and a purpose.

Here's what Christianity offers as an answer to this question: Christians believe that we exist to be an image of God in the world through our body-soul unity, for this is our nature. The Baltimore Catechism put it succinctly: "We are called to know, love, and serve God in this world so as to live with him forever in the next." That's our end goal—that's why we're here. *How* we accomplish such an amazing calling will be as varied as each one of us. Some of us are natural technicians; others, designers; and others, gifted in the practices of counseling, healing, or law. But insofar as we exist, we are good and we are known and loved by God the Father.

If you interview random people on the street about what they want in life, the common human sentiment underneath any desire for money or fame is, "I want to be happy." But few people know how to achieve that happiness, especially if it's believed that we are random products of an impersonal universe. The false avenues to happiness we all chase after (pleasure, wealth, popularity, and power) are not bad in themselves, but if we pursue them as the *ultimate* good (treating them as if they were God), they will never be enough to satisfy—because they never can and were never made to.

Furthermore, happiness as a goal is a fleeting reality. We all want to be happy, but happiness is a by-product of something else: providing a meal for your family, giving a gift to someone unexpectedly, or excelling in a talent you have that brings life to others. You can never *permanently* stay in a state of happiness, for there *will be* suffering and heartache and loss in this world. We must honestly face those realities. As priest and author Monsignor Charles Murray wrote, "The good life should allow people to work at things that are personally satisfying and expressive of themselves. . . . The good life should include also a certain leisure [that] is the basis of human culture. There should be opportunities to contribute to the common good as well as to pursue personal happiness. There should be time for family and friends, for worship and prayer."[5]

A good life, then, is a life lived in balance with all our responsibilities, one that is attentive to our nature and call as created by God. It is a life in which a person can enjoy the things of this world—food, athletics, relationships, and video games—without worshiping those things as ends in themselves. It is a life that is attuned to others and seeks to serve them because, as we'll explore later, we only come to find who we are when we become a gift to another person. And *that* is where a good life becomes a heroic one.

How do we live this good life though? It's not enough to merely intellectually grasp the concept. We must put these principles into action in order to become excellent and thus live well. For this, we need the virtues.

VIRTUE AND EXCELLENCE

"Man, you're really good at this game!" So I was told as I schooled every one of my dormmates in *Mario Kart 64*. I could run laps around my buddies and had every course down to a T. I thought I was the master—until Alvaro walked in.

Alvaro had never played with us before. He didn't seem interested in games as a whole, but he asked if he could join us one evening. Pleasantly surprised, we all welcomed him in. He muttered something about playing this game "occasionally with his brother," but I didn't think anything of it. Arrogantly, I didn't think much of this newcomer who had just entered my domain.

What happened next was a bloodbath. Alvaro unlocked some dormant muscle memory of the game that left our jaws on the floor as he proceeded to dominate *every* single racetrack. My puffed-up demeanor changed to desperation as I tried everything I could to no avail. I will never forget my friend Philip who dropped his controller, literally rolling-laughing on the floor at my misfortune. Alvaro had perfected every single shortcut and every turn, and there was nothing I could do to stop him. With a perfect landing of the "Big Jump" on Rainbow Road, Alvaro won every race of every cup of the game.

Flustered but defeated, and my pride severely shattered, we all had nothing but admiration and awe for the mild-mannered Alvaro who had clearly practiced *Mario Kart* to the point of perfection. For Alvaro, casual play had become an ingrained habit, which became utter mastery of the game. No one dared to challenge Alvaro again.

We all switched over to *Halo* the following week.

OUR HABITS MAKE US

The habits we create end up creating who we are. We all know and have experienced this to some degree. Repeated actions become our habits. We start a daily rhythm of brushing our teeth at the same time, exercising, and eating healthy, and eventually these actions become a part of ourselves. We can establish poor habits too, such as never accomplishing our work, stealing from others, or using crude language without thought. Our repeated habits, which are our dispositions to behave in a certain way, shape the person we are becoming.

Aristotle gave attention to the virtues as a way of living the happiest life possible (a state called *eudaimonia*). The *virtues* are simply habits of excellence (as opposed to the *vices*, which are habits of poor behavior). Rather than merely following external rules or chasing those false metrics of happiness (wealth or popularity), happiness lies in being a person of excellent habits, for the virtues shape our character and lead us toward living the good life—the best life possible.

A deep dive into the virtues is beyond the scope of this book, and some virtues will be examined later in the text, but let's quickly survey the four cardinal and three theological virtues. The traditional four cardinal virtues are fortitude, temperance, justice, and prudence. Fortitude is courage, doing the right thing even when it's difficult. Temperance is the ability to regulate our desires and say no to the things we enjoy. Justice is "giving another his or her due"—the responsibility I owe to others: God, strangers, and friends. Prudence is the charioteer that directs all the other behaviors and keeps them in balance; prudence allows us "to discern our true good in every circumstance and to choose the right means of achieving it" (*CCC*, 1806).

The three theological virtues, introduced by Christianity, are faith, hope, and love (or charity). They are ultimately gifts (graces) from God; we can't will them through our own hard work. We gain them through an open heart that offers God the chance to act in and through us. Faith is the virtue that believes in and ascends to the word of God. Hope is not optimism, but the virtue by which we desire God's kingdom and trust in Christ's promises (*CCC*, 1817); hope keeps us from discouragement in times of struggle, knowing that God is faithful. By love (charity), we mean the virtue of putting God's love into action and willing the good for others even when it requires sacrifice.

You sadly can't become virtuous by merely reading a book about the virtues, just as you can't become a great athlete if you never actually practice the sport. Stories and games that display heroes we admire can inspire us, but we become courageous by *doing* courageous things consistently. We grow in temperance as we learn to say no to the things that tempt us (even good things, such as candy or gaming for "just one more round"). We grow in love when we consistently set aside what *we* want to do in order to serve another. With the help of God's grace above all, we can learn to become better men and women through our small, daily actions. The good life becomes a heroic life when we make unselfishness a habit—when we love freely.

Dr. Edward Sri, a prominent author and presenter on the Catholic faith, sums up why living in a virtuous way matters for us today: "In short, virtue gives us the freedom to love. To the extent we lack generosity, patience, courage, and self-control, we will do selfish, impatient, cowardly, and out-of-control things that will hurt other people. But the more we grow in these and other virtues, the more we will have the ability to love the people in our lives the way they deserve to be loved."[6]

YOUR SOUL FULLY ALIVE

Now, I love downing a box of Cheez-Its and gaming until 1 a.m. as much as anyone, but I know there are consequences to my activity.

I wake up the next day feeling groggy and sluggish. When I eat clean and acknowledge my body's need for sleep, I tend to operate much better. So it's up to me to build habits that allow me to be at my best so I can show up for the people I love and the work I'm called to do.

These kinds of habits are important for our whole selves—not just our bodies. To be at our best—to strive for heroism—we have to attend to habits that form our *entire* human person, not just our gut. Striving for heroic excellence (virtue) is literally what will make us the happiest and "most ourselves" people we can be. Truly, the *healthiest* thing for us is to be the *holiest* version of ourselves.

Here's a fun word that we've largely lost use of: *magnanimous*. It's a mouthful, but it sums up how we're called to be in the world: men and women striving for heroism. *Magnanimous* literally means being "of great soul." It's a word that reminds us that our greatness is found not in puffed-up arrogance but in knowing who we are, with all our strengths and weaknesses, and to whom we belong.

To be a person of magnanimity means that I know my worth and dignity, and can hold my head up high and say, "I know that I am fallen, but God loves me and has redeemed me, and I have something to offer the world." As St. Ireneaus, a Greek bishop in the second century, tells us, "The glory of God is man fully alive!" When we become the fully unique individuals that we are and live as such, we give God the highest praise. When we are living virtuously, and seeking not comfort or false goods but a life lived in accord with what is best for us, we are living "the good life" indeed.

When I think of my own children (my wife and I have five on earth and three in heaven), I want them to be the unique, quirky, weird people that they are. Some of my kids are musical, others are natural artists, some have an amazing sense of humor and comedic timing, and others have a born athletic prowess. I don't want them to become clones of other people; I want them to be *fully* them. As it brings joy to my fatherly heart, so too does it delight God when we live well, guided by virtue, in full freedom. Jesus did not come to give us rules and make us miserable, but as he acclaimed, "I came that they may have life, and have it abundantly" (Jn 10:10).

WHERE TO NOW?

"Am I a good man?" "Am I a good woman?"

These are deceptively simple questions that should provoke profound reflection. It's what many people ask as they approach the twilight of their lives: "Did I live a good life?" "Did I help others enough?" "Did I spend my time well?"

Hopefully our answer will be a resounding YES! "Yes, I helped others." "Yes, I spent my time well with those whom I love." "Yes, I lived a good life." And if we haven't been on that trajectory, every day is a chance to start anew and make small decisions to start building up new habits and growing in virtue. For we are indeed called to go beyond ourselves and live this life in an excellent, magnanimous, and even heroic way.

"We all, on some level, wish to surrender our individual selves to what Freud referred to as the 'oceanic' feeling of belonging to something greater," writes psychologist Alexander Kriss.[7] Throughout time and across religions (and lack thereof), there's a common ache of the human heart for this greatness, a universal desire to enter into and achieve it. Even atheist psychologists like Sigmund Freud couldn't escape naming that longing of human existence that pulls at each one of us, calling us to "do more" with our lives.

But *where* did it come from? *Who* put it there in the first place? Let's press forward into these questions in the chapter ahead.

QUESTIONS FOR REFLECTION

- Do you believe that you are called to greatness? Why or why not?

- In what areas of life do you tend to fall into comfort or laziness?

- What virtues would you like to grow in? What habits do you think might help you grow in these virtues?

3

WHAT DOES GAMING HAVE TO DO WITH GOD?

Think of individuals whose contributions shaped their field forever: Thomas Edison with electricity, Henry Ford with the automobile, and Steve Jobs with smartphones. This is who Shigeru Miyamoto is to the video game industry.

Hired as a staff artist by Nintendo in 1977 at the age of twenty-four, Miyamoto established himself by creating the game *Donkey Kong*, where the hero climbed ladders and dodged projectiles to defeat a stubborn gorilla and rescue the fair maiden. Miyamoto designed the plucky plumber, originally called "Jumpman" (since his job was literally hopping over barrels), but later renamed him Mario. Nintendo's mascot was born!

Miyamoto went on to develop the original *Super Mario Bros.* and *The Legend of Zelda*, and he would later design titles such as *Star Fox*, *Pikmin*, and the racing game *F-Zero*. Overseeing these successful franchises and creating some of the most recognizable video game characters in the world, Miyamoto put the Nintendo company on the map and cemented his place in the history of the gaming industry. A joyful, humble, and endlessly curious man, Miyamoto currently continues to imagine what's next for video game experiences, even though he is past the age of seventy.

I know my life has been affected by Miyamoto's creations, and I'm willing to bet yours has as well. My childhood practically follows the evolution of the *Mario, Zelda,* and *Donkey Kong* games—from sixteen-bit, side-scrolling sprites to fully rendered and graphically glorious worlds. The first time I played *Super Mario 64* and realized that I could explore the world in 360 degrees, going wherever I wanted to go, my smile stretched from ear to ear across my middle school braces. Now I'm making new memories with my own kids as they discover these characters for the first time, and I find myself marveling at how one person's imagination can affect the world.

All that to say, if there's a game, there must be a game designer, someone who first playfully imagined and then constructed the creation into being.

THE UNDESIGNED GAME DESIGNER

Allow me to put all my cards on the table: I am a Catholic Christian man. I believe that God exists. I believe he has revealed himself, and we can know him in a deep and beautiful way. After a long journey of wandering about in our culture and asking all the questions of the major world religions, I believe that I am known and loved by God uniquely through the person of Jesus Christ—and that you, dear reader, are as well.

If you'd like to close the book at this point, you are free to do so. But I invite you to press on and see if what I share resonates with how you have experienced reality. I believe that video games, at their best, echo the fact that we are willed into existence and loved by a Creator who desires for us not a life of monochrome boredom but one of expansive greatness. There's a great adventure you've been invited into, and I hope you ask some of the hard questions that give our life meaning.

If we ask the question, "Does God even exist?" we must admit this starting point: *I did not create myself.* We are all dependent on something outside of us to be here. That chain of dependency goes on and on until it must hit a point of origin. Nothing begins in and of itself—everything originates by being acted upon by an outside force. For instance, a rack of pool balls cannot and will not move unless acted on by an outside pool player. A video game cannot be created without a designer and a development team.

Now, some argue that the universe is cyclical, such as in Buddhist thought, and that there's an endless cycle of death and rebirth. But even within such a system, we still have not answered that stubborn question of "How did it all begin?" A closed-loop system still needs something outside of it to kick-start it into motion and maintain its existence.

Consider, too, the very order of the cosmos. Chaos cannot create order; only order can beget order. In observing nature and the ordered universe, scientists, poets, and artists throughout the centuries have marveled at the coherence of all that exists. Albert Einstein once observed, "The most incomprehensible thing about the universe is its comprehensibility." If the universe weren't constant and ordered, we could never conduct repeatable, scientific experiments or move to a deeper knowledge of anything. We could never study and make something coherent out of continual chaos. St. Athanasius, a bishop of the fourth century, wrote, "If the movement of the universe were irrational, and the world rolled on in random fashion, one would be justified in disbelieving what we say. But if the world is founded on reason, wisdom, and science, and is filled with orderly beauty, then it must owe its origin and order to none other than the Word of God."[1]

The original *Donkey Kong* simply didn't magically pop into existence or fall from the sky—it arose from the creative mind of Shigeru Miyamoto. Something does not, and cannot, emerge from nothing. It takes something (or someone) to create something or someone. Aristotle called this point of origination the "unmoved mover." St. Thomas Aquinas agreed, teaching that we need a first cause. And for men and women of religious belief, we call that someone "God."

This is all simple logic, but we're living in an era where religious belief is often ridiculed or mocked as something absurd. But if you found pebbles that spelled out "Help!" on a beach, the absurd thought would be "Wow, random ocean tides and winds made these pebbles to spell out such words." The quite sane response would be, "*Who* wrote this?"

No one could watch some of the masterpiece games of our day, such as *The Last of Us* or *God of War,* and think, "Oh yeah, that game randomly came into existence." Similarly, it would take great mental gymnastics to look about at the cosmos, hear the music of Beethoven or John Williams, or look into the eyes of a baby and think, "This is all from random atoms colliding, and there's no meaning to any of it."

The perfectly sane response to a universe of such beauty, to a planet that's the exact tilt and dimensional length and distance from the sun to support life, and to a species that can act in freedom and intelligence is, "Who made this?"

BUT WHAT IS GOD?

Back to the question of God—what is God? God is not a thing or even the "highest thing" in the created universe; he's not a "flying spaghetti monster" or an indifferent old man with a beard at the edge of the galaxy. God is not a policeman waiting to catch us whenever we behave poorly, a magical Santa who grants our wishes like an ATM, or a tyrant who is threatened by us and thus diminishes us at every turn to keep us in check.

Most people rebel against God because their conception of him is one of the caricatures listed above—they never moved beyond a third-grade idea of him. As it turns out, *none* of those images sum up what we as Catholic Christians mean by "God."

Fr. Damian Ference writes, "God has no need to compete with us because God is God. . . . Before anything ever existed, God existed. God has no beginning or end. God just is. God is not a thing—God is God. Thomas Aquinas called God the sheer act of existence. God is existence itself."[2] This is the reason for the cryptic name God reveals to Moses in the Exodus account of the burning bush: "I AM WHO I AM" (Ex 3:14).

Or in layman's terms: "I am Being itself. I always was, am now, and forever will be."

That's heavy. It's also a beautifully simple reality. God is a mystery, a reality we can never fully wrap our human minds around. It's like an ant trying to comprehend an elephant. God is not an impersonal force either but a divine unity of persons. The even more astounding thing is that this Supreme Being would actually want us to know him in a close and intimate way and provide the means for this encounter to happen.

Deists believe that God is like a divine watchmaker who wound up the universe but really has no interaction with it after setting it in motion. While many in our culture believe some version of deism today—that if God exists, he's like some far-off uncle who just wants me to be nice and live my life—it is a shallow way of thinking about God, given everything we know about him from scripture and our tradition. It is, however, an easier way to think about God because it allows us to have a relationship with him that does not ask anything of us. I had to lay aside this misconception myself and admit that this flawed understanding of God was keeping me from entering into the mystery of a relationship with him.

St. John knew, walked with, and wrote about Jesus almost two thousand years ago. He knew that faith is not about following blind rules but about entering into an explosive story of love: "He who does not love does not know God; for God is love. In this the love of God was made manifest among us, that God sent his only Son into the world, so that we might live through him. In this is love, not that we loved God but that he loved us and sent his Son to be the expiation for our sins. Beloved, if God so loved us, we also ought to love one another" (1 Jn 4:8–11).

A relationship with God through faith is not something that will fit nicely into a textbook. It is a mystery—but that doesn't mean we throw up our hands because we can't know anything about it. Nor does it mean that it's a riddle to be solved. To say that God is a mystery simply means that we cannot *come to the end* of knowing him—he is always beyond us. To develop a relationship with God means accepting that faith will invite us into ever deeper waters and take us places beyond what we can imagine for ourselves.

WE ARE ENCODED WITH GOD'S IMAGE

God doesn't simply exist—he also *creates*. Not because he had to or because he was bored, but it was out of love and generosity that God created everything to be, to exist. God wills the cosmos and all in it into existence out of nothing. "The highest things often have 'footprints,' as the medievals put it, among the lower things," wrote professor and author Fr. James Schall.[3] As an artist often leaves a hidden signature within their painting or sculpture, so too can we perceive the fingerprint of God throughout creation—especially in ourselves as men and women, a species beyond anything else in the whole of creation.

We are persons because we've been made in the image and likeness of God, who has revealed himself to be not one but three persons—Father, Son, and Holy Spirit. This is what Christians mean by the Trinity. We've been made in the image of this communion, this loving family of persons. This is why all the great stories (and the very best video game stories) constantly come back to the theme of family, love, and sacrifice. It's in our very DNA.

Being created in the "image and likeness" of God means that we have a dignity and worth like no other creature. God is rational and capable of love, and thus so are we. And we are "the only creature on earth that God has willed for its own sake," calling us "to share, by knowledge and love, in God's own life" (*CCC*, 356). This is really mind-blowing stuff if we stop to take in this concept!

THE STORIES WE'RE IN

Among the most fundamental ancient characteristics of humanity is the desire to tell a story. For proof, one need only look at the great cave paintings of Lascaux in southern France.[4] Thousands of years before cities and armies, people painted pictures of ordinary life: animals, nature, and members of the family are etched in pastel markings in the caverns of stone. These cave walls inspired archeologists to interpret these and other discoveries as evidence of the emergence of a new, distinctly *human* consciousness that did not exist prior. Clearly, from the very beginning of our humanity, we value storytelling.

That primeval drive of the caveman from Lascaux remains in the heart of every person. We love stories because we are conscious of life and eager to hear how others experience it. Thus, all of recorded history is accompanied by the tales of victory and defeat, love and hatred, war and conquest, and profanity and divinity. We want to know how and why things happen, and stories are often the way of transmitting this information, as well as our heroes and the moral lessons they embody, to the next generation.

"I had always felt life first as a story: and if there is a story there is a story-teller," noted the journalist and author G. K. Chesterton.[5]

If God is indeed the supreme storyteller, and we have been made in the image and likeness of him, then of course we *love* stories. We love hearing and making up our own stories. Jesus himself constantly taught in parables and analogies, knowing that the information conveyed in a story is always received more willingly than bland instruction or PowerPoint presentations. We lean forward when a story is told, wanting to hear "What's next?" And the best of stories always echo God's story of self-sacrificial love, the love that moved Christ to die for us on the Cross, the hero who loved to the point of giving up his life.

The video game industry is an avid competitor to Hollywood's own storytelling. Early games dealt with basic themes like beating the bad guy and saving the world. But we now see game designers tackling more serious stories, diving into profound subject matter, and creating three-dimensional characters with voice actors who match the best in Hollywood. Gaming has evolved from a means of entertainment to a form of art that expresses the deeper questions about human existence. Games like the *BioShock* franchise offer profound reflections on free will and the destructive allure of utopia; the *Uncharted* games show the existential tension in preserving family against the beckoning of "just one more" adventure. Many games even offer alternate endings, based on your choices and how you behaved. Gaming is one of the only mediums, outside of real life, where I am an active part of the story and therefore I must take seriously the part given to me.

THE ADVENTURE AHEAD

Being raised in a small town within Kyoto, Japan, Shigeru Miyamoto was an endlessly curious child, opening every cupboard and exploring nearby fields. *The Legend of Zelda* series is a unique hybrid of Miyamoto's love of traditional fantasy—specifically J. R. R. Tolkien's *The Lord of the Rings*—and the dopamine rush of finding something new under every stone. Recalling his inspiration for *Zelda*'s emphasis on exploration, Miyamoto explained, "When I was a child, I went hiking and found a lake. It was quite a surprise for me to stumble upon it. When I travelled around the country without a map, trying to find my way, stumbling on amazing things as I went, I realized how it felt to go on an adventure like this."[6]

In speaking about Link, the protagonist of the *Zelda* games, Miyamoto affirmed the elemental nature of our call into the unknown, to confront great odds, and to embrace the hero's journey. "Link is a normal boy, but he has a destiny to fight great evil. Many people dream about becoming heroes."[7] Indeed, in all the great games, we can paint a bit of ourselves onto the hero because we all want to pursue the greatness we have within ourselves. And it's God who placed that call on our hearts in the first place.

To be human is to be created and invited into a grand adventure! We exist, and it is good that we are here! If we feel stirred to great things, great challenges, great friendships, and a love story that matters, it is because the God who created us desires for us to participate in these things and seek them out. So will you say yes to that challenge?

Let's "level up" in the chapters ahead to examine the deeper stirrings in our hearts and how the heroic life is lived with a radical yes to all that God has in store for us.

QUESTIONS FOR REFLECTION

- Do you believe that God exists? Why or why not?

- If so, how do you relate to him—how do you share your life with him and experience his life in you?

- What has been your experience with religion or spirituality?

- Have you ever envisioned your life as a story? What thoughts do you have about this way of looking at life?

LEVEL 2

4

IDENTITY, MISSION, AND COMMUNITY

I mentioned at the beginning of this book that I was a skinny fellow (my uncle's nickname for me was Beanpole) and not very good at any sports that involved catching, throwing, or anything involving a ball, so video games were often my refuge. But I was a natural swimmer and did pretty well for myself during my swim club and high school years. Swimming gave me plenty of time to think, staring at that black line at the bottom of the pool, and it also gave me a frame of reference to appreciate some of the most hardworking athletes of all, the Olympians.

With the rest of America, I eagerly watched Michael Phelps dominate the pool at the Olympic games from the summer of 2004 through his last swims in Brazil in 2016. In between two of his later games though, Phelps experienced repeated DUIs from his participation in the party and pot lifestyle, and ended up in a rehab center for addiction. I remember thinking, "Man, this guy has it all! He's on top of the world with his success. Why would he self-sabotage?"

In an interview after his exit from rehab, Phelps admitted that he suffered a long bout with anxiety and depression and was even considering suicide. "I thought the world would just be better off without me," Phelps said. "I figured that was the best thing to do— just end my life."[1]

Beyond the grind of his sport, Phelps didn't have a *purpose*. Yes, he "had it all," but like many men and women who gain all the coveted things of this earth—money, power, pleasure, and fame—it can never and will never satisfy that restless "God-shaped hole."

At Phelps's lowest point, athlete and friend Ray Lewis, linebacker from the Baltimore Ravens, gave the champion swimmer Rick Warren's Christian bestseller *The Purpose Driven Life*. Warren's book has sold millions of copies since it was published in 2002, and though the book approaches large themes from a religious perspective, it has resonated with many, regardless of their faith. Many athletes and celebrities have been moved by Warren's manuscript, and Phelps was potentially even saved by it. Lewis said in an interview, "I basically told him, 'Okay, everything has a purpose, and now, guess what? It's time to wake up.'"

In an ESPN special, Phelps stated that the book "turned me into believing that there is a power greater than myself and there is a purpose for me on this planet" and "helped me when I was in a place that I needed the most help."[2] It even spurred him to reconcile with his dad, whom he had been estranged from since childhood.

Phelps finished his swimming career in 2016 with twenty-eight Olympic medals, twenty-three of them being gold. His mission in the pool being accomplished, he has moved on to a place of willingness to share his experience with depression and now advocates for greater mental health awareness so that others might know that their lives also have meaning and they are not alone.

MY PURPOSE HERE ON EARTH

What does Phelps's story have to do with us and our consideration of God and video games in our lives? Well, here's the thing—regardless of your background, religion, or level of athleticism, our hearts are made to know three central things: our identity ("Who am I?"), our mission ("What's my purpose?"), and our community ("Who is with me?").

These are the questions that haunt and beckon us all, whether we are gamers or not, athletes or not, or rich and famous or not. They are the most important questions in life! While many choose to ignore or suppress these deep prompts of existence, we all have to face these questions eventually. Even choosing not to answer them is a way of answering them and could lead to a disastrous outcome.

If even Michael Phelps, at the height of his career with worldwide fame, could feel the emptiness of a life without a higher purpose, none of us are exempt either.

To be human is to be created and invited into a grand adventure! It is good that we are here, participating in life and existence. And it is good that you are here. Your life is important and you matter.

If we feel stirred to great things, great challenges, great friendships, and a love story that matters, it is because the God who created us desires for us to participate in these things and seek them out in life. And if we feel called to gaming, it is because we have a Creator who delights in this back-and-forth act of play. If we have been created in the image and likeness of God who playfully creates (think of the humor it took to create the giraffe or the platypus), it's no surprise that people continue to create new board games, apps, and indie games every single day.

Video game developers and companies, to some degree, understand the importance of addressing these deep human needs of identity, mission, and community. We might even feel that these cries of our hearts are heard and given a reprieve through games more than through our church communities. So let's break each of these three core questions down, beginning with the very starting point of our being: our identity.

IDENTITY: WHO AM I?

"I know who I am. I'm Steve!"

This was from a wisecracking freshmen football player who thought he sufficiently answered the question that has plagued humanity since Socrates. I allowed the classroom to settle down, and I met his self-satisfied smile with my own response.

"Yes, Steve. We all know your *name*. But who *are* you?"

Steve looked at me as if I had three heads. At least he was listening, even if I temporarily broke his brain. The rest of the classroom was silent, as they realized I was serious. I proceeded in my gentle interrogation.

"Who are you if you get injured and can't play football again?" I asked. "Who are you if you don't get into the college of your choice? Who are you, without the safety net of your family, or your group of friends, or that phone you stare into for all hours of the day? Steve, who are *you*?"

I let the questions hang for about five seconds of silence that seemed like fifty. Steve finally spoke up:

"I don't know, Mr. Angel."

"Good, Steve." I smiled. "Now we can begin."

"I AM...?"

Who we are is constantly changing. I am the same Bobby I was from my mother's womb, and yet I am also *not* the same person I was at age two. Who I am now as a husband and father is quite different than who I was during college. Even at the bodily level, our cells are constantly turning over, dying and replicated anew, so that a percentage of our cellular being is something different than before. (For a fun thought experiment on this conundrum, look up the "Ship of Theseus," which ponders whether an object that has had all of its original components replaced remains the same object.)

Oftentimes we wrap up our identity in our career or profession. Among men in particular, the follow-up question to any introduction of our names is usually, "What do you *do*?" We often place importance on our job or what school we were admitted to, but all sorts of secondary aspects of our life can stake the claim on our core personhood.

Sometimes we place our identity in our sport, hobby, ethnicity, or where we fall on the spectrum of our sexual attractions. "I identify as _____" or "_____ is who I *am*," we declare. Now, some of these aspects of your life are important (and some are not), and some will even change as you grow through life. Some elements are more core to the substance of your humanity than others, but all of these components can never encompass the full mystery of who you are.

"I am a mystery even to myself," wrote mystic and Franciscan friar St. Padre Pio, who knew his gifts and position before God quite well.[3] And yet, even he could leave room for mystery and God's grace. There's a sacred, interior portion within each of us that another can never fully understand or participate in. Sometimes we're fickle and do the things we don't want to do; sometimes we surprise ourselves, and moments of courage and greatness shine through.

This is part of being made in the mysterious image of God in the messy unity of body and soul.

That being said, we *need* to have some settled concept of who we are in order to function in the world. I also cannot *offer* the world anything if I don't know who I am. So while I may never know the depths of who God has created me to be as Bobby, I know that I *am* Bobby and that I am unique, unrepeatable, and have something to offer the world.

Particularly during the teenage years, we desire to individuate ourselves and learn who we are apart from our parents and household. We try on a few hats with new tribes who have new fashions and listen to new music. Developmental psychologists have noted that the crucial conflict of adolescence is one between establishing a stable identity and the mire of role confusion. Ideally, in our teenage years we learn how to regulate emotions, handle responsibilities, and contribute to society; we can emerge from this period of testing with a grounded sense of who we are.

But we can just as likely get "stuck" in adolescent patterns of self-absorption and relational dysfunction, and thus feel utterly unprepared to meet the challenges of adult life. With the revolution of smartphones and social media apps, the cultural breakdown of the family, and the Western world's lack of rites of passage into maturity, our generation struggles with this fundamental question of adolescence: "Who am I?" This is certainly the cry of our generation, cut off from a grander historical narrative and aimless as we grasp for any sense of purpose.

Here is where video games provide at least a temporary answer to this crucial question of the heart.

MY AVATAR IS ME

Consider that any story, novel, or film that engages me is naturally having me identify with its protagonist and live vicariously through them. When I watch *Gladiator*, I am seeing the world through the eyes of Maximus Decimus Meridius, feeling his story and "putting on" the character's emotions and life in their time period (and feeling extra manly by the story's end—*are you not entertained*?!). Video games do the same at a potentially even more visceral degree because

I'm actually *controlling* that protagonist, moving them around in their world, exploring and creating, and even dying. The game becomes (or appears to become) the player's story. The avatar is simply a vessel by which the player can enact his or her will in the virtual world.

(An "avatar," by the way, is an icon or figure representing a particular person in video games: Mario, Sonic, Master Chief, your Pokémon catcher, or the Sim you created and have gotten overly attached to. It's the character you're moving around with your joystick or keyboard. The word *avatar* comes from the Hindu concept of a manifestation of a deity in bodily form on earth—the word translates to "descent." We can see this concept of an avatar in the pixelated character on the screen—it's not me, and yet I am exerting my will *through* this character.)

Maybe we aren't happy with who we are. Maybe we think "the grass would be greener" and life would be better if we were someone else. We all have parts of ourselves we can pick apart and find dissatisfaction with: our height, weight, physical features, habits, or quirks. Maybe we think we'll be happier if we could become a totally new person. Here's where video games can offer a temporary, perhaps even healthy, solution to the curiosity of wondering what life would be like "outside of me." In games, I get to be a warrior, a treasure hunter, a soldier, or even a silly creature like a hedgehog or gorilla wearing a necktie.

As the games have progressed, the options for customizing our avatars have increased exponentially. Certain games have options for facial hair, clothing, weaponry, and even tattoos. Millions of gamers turn to video games for a sense of personal development. In games such as *Second Life*, *The Sims*, and *Bloodborne*, players can customize their own characters with unique personalities. These avatars are outlets for self-expression and a sense of identity.

Now, at the benign end, there's nothing wrong with the creation of these kinds of "alternate selves" to enjoy the play of the game and allow our imaginations to run wild. In a sense, it's almost like acting out a character, only the stage is on a screen. The problem is when we start to *prefer* our online digital avatar to our real-life, incarnate selves. If we find ourselves so dissatisfied with life around us (and even our very bodies) and fail to see where we fit into the world, we will naturally start to prefer our virtual lives over our flesh-and-blood ones.

MISSION: I HAVE A PURPOSE

"Only you can slay the dragon!"

"What are you waiting for? Get up and go save my chickens!"

"I sure hope no one wanders into the ghost castle beyond those bushes . . ."

We all have heard some kind of version of these directional pleas in games old and new from the poor nonplayable character (NPC) who is walking in circles and imploring our help. Whether it's defeating a beast, solving a puzzle, or rescuing some lost chickens, video games offer a very clear sense of purpose to gamers: you can make a difference here, and you are needed. "This town needs *me!*"

Many people today feel frustrated because they feel their lives have no purpose and that they don't have a clear sense that they're making a meaningful change. Before the lockdowns of the COVID-19 pandemic, researchers were already sounding the alarm on the declining mental health of young people. In 2019, *Time* magazine reported that "between 2009 and 2017, rates of depression among kids ages 14 to 17 increased by more than 60%," citing a study published in the *Journal of Abnormal Psychology*, further noting that "the CDC has also issued reports showing that rates of suicide among young people jumped 56% between 2007 and 2016."[4] In the Western world in particular, we've achieved a peak state of material and technological comfort but find ourselves spiritually and psychologically emptier than ever.

"When a man does not know what harbor he is making for, no wind is the right wind."[5] These words from the Roman philosopher Seneca are just as relevant today as they were nineteen hundred years ago. Young adulthood is a season of life full of energy, yet so few of us have clear outlets to focus that energy—it is so easy to lack purpose and direction. This naturally leads to a sense of helplessness, confusion, and despair. But in the absence of a purpose in the greater world, where *can* I go to feel like I matter and have something to offer? Video games.

THE IMPORTANCE OF QUEST

"Game designers and game researchers have learned interesting things about humans and their roles," writes Indiana University professor of media Dr. Edward Castranova. "People want to be heroes. They crave agency, and the ability to do something that matters. They want meaning."[6] We all want to feel we're contributing something to the world. When a culture strips away any acknowledgment of God and objective meaning, our ache for purpose must go somewhere, and for many, that human need is quenched by video games. "Quests are essential to a life well-lived," writes Castranova. "They solidify our sense that we have something to do, our sense of purpose. Without quests, life would be terribly boring."[7] In other words, our modern-day problem is that we have lost our quests.

Video games, specifically those that provide prodigious quests and adventures, tap into the innate longing for mission. And these missions are epic—outside of casual cell phone or sports games, "saving the world" seems to be a category all on its own. So-called AAA games that boast film-sized budgets and A-list voice actors draw players into immersive lands and feature plots that rival anything Hollywood has to offer. The best of these games, though, don't feature spectacle for the sake of spectacle. Rather, they draw players into wonder as they traverse vast lands and enter into stories that matter. Every gamer has a role to play. Games that invite us to save the world help us experience a unique kind of power: the power to accomplish something meaningful.[8]

Gamers are actively involved in the story of a game, not solely passive recipients of a movie, and thus it feels as if the actions within the virtual world have real meaning because, well, they do! The world depends on you! When we're caught up in the awe of an epic story, we know we're also involved in a story bigger than ourselves. We're drawn in by beauty and awe, and we experience the important desire to serve and grow past our own self-interests.

GOD'S CALLING FOR YOU

The Greek term *telos* refers to the "end" or "final cause" of a thing (to draw from the thought of Aristotle and Aquinas). Essentially, the *telos* of a thing answers the question, "What's the purpose of this thing?"

Let's return to the example of a chair, for instance: What is the purpose of a chair? To be sat on, right? A chair that falls over or breaks when I attempt to sit on it is not fulfilling its purpose (*telos*). It is failing at its mission to be a chair.

What's the *telos* of the human person? What are we created *for*? Why are we here? Our society has largely thrown away this question because if we leave that question unanswered, we can follow any desire we want. But in our heart of hearts, we experience a restlessness—a drive to serve a purpose, to contribute to something meaningful. And God has placed that restlessness within our hearts so that we won't truly rest until we know *why* we're here and what we're made *for*.

Consider this beautiful passage from the *Catechism of the Catholic Church* on our common *telos* as human beings: "God put us into the world to know, to love, and to serve him, and so to come to paradise. Beatitude [happiness] makes us 'partakers of the divine nature' and of eternal life. With beatitude, man enters into the glory of Christ and into joy of the Trinitarian life" (1721). These three sentences sum up the beauty of why we are here. We're not just brought into this existence out of love by God; we are also bestowed with a vocation (from *vocare*: "to call"), a mission or destiny in this life. Our ultimate goal is to see God face-to-face, a theological concept we call the "beatific vision." But before that time (God willingly) comes, we all have different tasks or callings upon this earth to share the good news of God's love for us. Some of us are called to marriage; some, to religious orders or the priesthood. Some will feel called to be missionaries, others are called to professional life, and some might be called to do good work in the digital space as designers, composers, or streamers.

You have a purpose and a mission in the time you've been given on earth. Mission comes from *missio*, which means "to be sent." In his seminal work, *Man's Search for Meaning*, Holocaust survivor Viktor Frankl writes, "Everyone has his own specific vocation or mission in life to carry out a concrete assignment which demands fulfillment. Therein he cannot be replaced, nor can his life be repeated. Thus, everyone's task is as unique as is his specific opportunity to implement it."[9]

Meaning, purpose, direction, quest, vocation—men and women can put up with great suffering and tediousness and pain when we feel that we're moving toward something and we have something to offer the world. And the beautiful truth is that we are indeed being offered a great quest for our lives. We only need the new eyes to see it.

COMMUNITY: MADE FOR OTHERS

One of the world's most famous psychological studies followed 268 men from their college days to old age. The lead psychologist, George Vaillant, observed a common experience among the happiest men: "love—full stop," noting that "70 years of evidence that our relationships with other people matter, and matter more than anything else in the world."[10] More than exercise, diet, or supplements, the quality of our human relationships is what determines our greatest fulfillment in the world.

"No man is an island," we are told by many of the spiritual writers, and for good reason. Even if we're introverted or attempt to live totally apart from other humans, we need connection with other people to be fully human and find meaning and purpose. There's a reason that solitary confinement is considered one of the most inhumane forms of imprisonment, and why prolonged captivity has driven people insane. Remember: we're created in the image and likeness of a God who is a community of persons—Father, Son, and Holy Spirit—so a life of being a "lone wolf" is contrary to our social nature.

FORTNITE: A CASE STUDY IN COMMUNITY

Speaking of islands, let's examine the massively popular online game *Fortnite*. One of the most popular games in the world, *Fortnite* is an open-world combat game where players are dropped onto an island to duke it out solo or as a team in order to be the last player standing. You collect weapons, build defenses, and can access a series of "skins" (character costumes). If you do well, you may even want to make your character bust out one of the countless dance moves and emote options. And you can play with people throughout the world if you are hooked up to the internet. Since its release on July 25, 2017, it has amassed more than one billion dollars in revenue, despite it being a "free to play" game.

Our yearning for communion is on full display in the world of *Fortnite* and other massively multiplayer online games (MMOs), even if it is unbeknownst to most gamers themselves. According to the gaming website Polygon, several factors make *Fortnite* so popular, the first of which is "sharable moments":

> Obviously, the game is fun. But what makes it enjoyable? First and foremost, Battle Royale [was] designed to be a blank slate for vivid personal stories. Once inside the game, it's easy to be swept up in the travails and adventures of your avatar. Every time that bus cruises over the island, a hundred narratives unfold. Some of them are as forgettable as "I opened the door to a house and someone blew me apart with a shotgun." Others are more textured. "When I achieved my first Victory Royale, I couldn't stop myself from recounting the whole story to my entire family."[11]

This is a game that taps into the desire to "be with" others. As we read the different narratives being typed on our screen or spoken to us through our headphones by other players, we are immediately drawn into a society of which my personal story is an integral part. The "I" of the self always finds a way out of the self and into relation with the "other" person.

Fortnite has also demonstrated how games today are spaces not merely to play together but also to socialize and chat. *New York Magazine*'s Brian Feldman speculated that *Fortnite* has more in common with social networks than with other video games: "*Fortnite*, by contrast, seems here to stay because it's modeled not as a series with annual installments, but as a persistent online world that's always under construction . . . the way to think about *Fortnite* isn't *Halo*, but Instagram. Not *Call of Duty*, but Snapchat."[12] There are metrics to brag about, seasons and content constantly updated to keep gameplay fresh and the dopamine flowing, and you may even be sharing the gamespace with celebrities like the rapper Drake. The point is, you're playing not in a solo vacuum but in a constantly updated gathering space alongside others.

"REAL FRIENDS"

There's often a false dichotomy given between "real" or "offline" friends and virtual connections. The line is blurry, as we all engage with people in varying degrees of intimacy across the spectrum of screen and skin. Some might think these virtual friendships "aren't real," but this can do a severe disservice to our genuine need for connection. As one student told me during the COVID-19 pandemic, "They locked everything down, and I wasn't allowed to go outside and play . . . video games were literally the only thing I could do with friends!"

"Some research suggests that online social relations are broader but shallower, while offline relations are fewer but more intimate," writes Robert Putnam in *Bowling Alone*, a book that documented the rise of loneliness in American culture. "As we compare virtual and real-life social connections, we must keep in mind that rarely are these two distinct categories."[13]

I think we can all glance around at society and see how the rise of technology—from the TV to the PlayStation and the smartphone—has radically shifted the way we spend time with one another today. Many people spend hours with "friends" on social media platforms but feel lonelier than ever. We are indeed meant for others—something inside of us knows that pixels can never replace the joy of rubbing physical elbows with someone whom we love. But this also doesn't mean that many friendships sustained or even forged online "aren't real" and that our online interactions can absolutely spill over beyond the virtual.

In 2020, a British teenager who suffered a seizure while gaming online was saved by his friend, an American, who called emergency services in the United Kingdom from five thousand miles away.[14] This is one dramatic example, but there are countless quieter moments of decent humanity shown between gamers. I know of a former student who was able to comfort a teammate from another country when he heard, over his headset, his friend's mother enter the room and state that his grandfather had died. The chat went quiet for a while until my student simply asked, "You OK, man?" Tears and heavy sighs were shared, and suddenly the space of mindless gaming became a sacred small group where these players could be there for one another.

We also use video games as a means to create and maintain friendships. In many MMOs, you can spend months and even years of your life journeying through countless adventures with the same teammates. This creates a powerful sense of community, especially as an anchor point if a friend moves away.

When one church community I know of started a young adult group, a survey was handed out asking participants to list three things they hoped to experience through the ministry. Without fail, the number one priority for every young adult was "community." Although it is true that every generation wants to experience a sense of belonging, the yearning is particularly strong today. We game together in part to meet this need, and this is a good and necessary facet of being fully human.

THE ADVENTURE AHEAD

Pokémon creator Satoshi Tajiri was obsessed with collecting insects as a kid. He grew up in a suburb of Tokyo and was saddened by the decline of insects he saw as the city kept industrializing. One day, he had a vision of the Gameboy's link cable, a simple cable that could connect two physical players together, with insects traveling across the thin wire.[15]

The rest is history. *Pokémon* became an international sensation that spanned video games, TV, toys, trading cards, and more. The games themselves are a wonderful mixture of discovery and turn-based battles, activating that part in each of us that loves collecting the "full set" and exploring the unseen parts of the world. "Gotta catch them all!" was the motto that captivated a generation, and the *Pokémon* franchise is still going strong.

Tajiri intentionally wanted children trading with each other, as in the early games where there were exclusive monsters to each version of the game (I had the "Red" version and my brother had the "Blue," so it did force us to play nicely together). What's more, like Miyamoto, Tajiri knew that we come alive in the adventure, exploring the unknown, and embracing community. For many people, this is what *Pokémon* represents—it's a game series that taps into our deepest longings as human persons.

We spent time in this chapter recognizing these very real human needs—identity, meaning and purpose, and community—to affirm where they are being addressed and met in the virtual world. Games like *Fortnite*, *Apex Legends*, *League of Legends*, *World of Warcraft*, and *The Elder Scrolls* tap into our need for community with their massive playgrounds for players to get lost in. We were made not for isolation but for adventure!

It's important to realize that God designed *you* with these cries upon your heart and they need to be examined and finally answered. In the next chapter, we're going to raise our sights a bit higher on a powerful, creative fingerprint that God leaves on the world and in the best of games—that is, the power of beauty.

QUESTIONS FOR REFLECTION

- How would you answer the question, "Who are you?" Under what hobbies or traits are you tempted to define yourself?

- What is your mission in life? What would you say your purpose is?

- Do you feel you are part of a healthy community? How do you meet that need for others in your life?

5

THE BEAUTIFUL BECKONS

The game starts with a girl. Her face comes into focus while an ephemeral chorus of violins plays suspensefully in the background. Holding a basket of flowers, the young woman with a brunette braid slowly walks into a busy street while the camera pans out farther and farther to show you a futuristic steampunk metropolis. After allowing a moment to take in the vastness of the polluted, futuristic cityscape, a game title appears on the screen: *Final Fantasy VII*. Then the camera zooms down to chase a train being overtaken by a band of mercenaries, and the gameplay finally begins.

Final Fantasy VII sealed the franchise's place in history when the 1997 game went on to sell more than 13.3 million copies worldwide; it was hailed as a creative and commercial work of genius. Three CDs' worth of story, thirty-two-bit polygonal graphics against beautiful prerendered backgrounds, a diverse cast of lovable characters, a seemingly endless world map, arguably the most famous (and traumatizing) video game deaths ever, and a musical score of memorable anthems all contributed to a cinematic experience that set new standards in the gaming industry. I remember plugging hours and hours into the game, often daydreaming about the characters while in school and grinding up my experience points to battle the toughest enemies the game had to offer.

Even as an updated remake has been rolled out on the powerful gaming engines of today, *Final Fantasy VII* continues to captivate a new generation of gamers, drawing them in primarily for one alluring reason: it is beautiful.

WHAT IS BEAUTY?

The aim of this book has been to show that living a life that is good can indeed be in harmony with a love for and appreciation of video games. The two are not at odds with one another, nor is enjoyment of gaming opposed to having deep faith and a relationship with the living God. God, who is the author of your life and is calling you to greatness, rightfully wants you to enjoy all the good things of this beautiful world.

To live a life that is good is to live in alignment with what is true, and we often stumble toward this knowledge by following the breadcrumbs of beauty.

We are all instinctively drawn to beauty. The beautiful things of the world captivate us: sunsets, cathedrals, musical compositions, film and games, and above all, the human face. Moments of beauty pierce our hearts and often reduce us to tears. Beautiful art and architecture can physically stop us as we find a silent invitation in symmetry and color for our eyes and souls to rest. Lovely melodies arrest us, bring us to our feet, and can awaken deep nostalgia and tears. Moments of profound humanity, such as military homecomings, births, baptisms, and weddings, demonstrate the beautiful in an embodied, raw authenticity. We love to participate in these types of experiences.

If we're going to live a good life, it will necessarily be one that is open to beauty. But what is it about beauty that allures us and invites us to follow?

So what *is* beauty, anyway?

In a similarly befuddling inquiry, St. Augustine muses on the difficulty of defining "time": "What then is time? If no one asks me, I know; if I want to explain it to a questioner, I do not know."[1] There's a similar mysterious, slippery element to describing beauty, for when asked to define it, we often stumble. "I know it when I see it!" we might say. While there is certainly a subjective element about the kinds of art, architecture, or music we might prefer, beauty rightfully understood is not something founded solely on individual inclination, such as my favorite ice-cream flavor or T-shirt. Beauty is not merely in the eye of the beholder . . . it is something *more*.

THE TRANSCENDENTALS: BEAUTY, GOODNESS, AND TRUTH

The Good, the True, and the Beautiful—these are what ancient philosophers called *transcendental* values. These are qualities of existence itself, and we are created with an innate ability to perceive them in the way we encounter creation. For instance, a dog doesn't stop to wonder at a rainbow. But *we* do because it points us toward one of these transcendental values. In other words, we experience the true, the good, and the beautiful in ways that strike to the heart of our being as human persons.

Let's look at the transcendental value of truth to explore this concept a bit. I have enjoyed the vast majority of the *Assassin's Creed* franchise, minus a few entries with bland protagonists or unfulfilling story arcs. There's just something about parkouring off rooftops and exploring ancient time periods, all while embroiled in a work of historical fiction with a masterpiece of a soundtrack, that just fills my heart.

Early on in the series, *Assassin's Creed* focused on two embattled forces, the Order of the Assassins and the Order of the Templars, and their struggle to keep the other in check. The protagonists of the games had this curious, recurring phrase that came from their creed: "Nothing is true, everything is permitted."

I remember one round of gameplay in which I thought to myself, "That's absurd . . . to state 'nothing is true' is to declare *that statement itself* as a truth." But I then happily preceded to turn my brain off and enjoy the rest of the game. The budding philosopher in me was picking up on something though: the self-refutation of the claim "nothing is true" is worth noting.

Truth is the property of being in accord with reality. To be good and live well means that we live in accordance with what is true. Now, truth is not a tricky thing—it's actually quite simple to grasp, but it's exceedingly difficult to live out.

Truth has become something of a landmine for our generation. Everyone has "their own truth," which makes a bit of a mockery out of truth. A thing simply cannot be "true for me and not for you." Gravity cannot be true for me but untrue for you (feel free to try that out). But, alas, this is the age we're living in—it is a time that Pope Benedict XVI described as a "dictatorship of relativism" when every person thinks that truth is relative to their own experience. There is no overarching "right" or "wrong" according to relativism—and thus there is also no meaning.

Some of the most infamous dictators of recent times embraced relativism. Adolf Hitler asserted that "there is no such thing as truth, either in the moral or in the scientific sense."[2] Benito Mussolini, the dictator of Italy during the Second World War, wrote, "Everything I have said and done in these last years is relativism. . . . The modern relativist infers that everybody has the right to create for himself his own ideology, and to attempt to enforce it with all the energy of which he is capable."[3] When we try to create our own little realities, we end up all living like little tyrants, instead of humbly surrendering ourselves to the objective nature of truth that is outside of us. And the irony is that we make moral judgments all the time, from condemning historical atrocities to disapproving of the hypocritical activities of our world leaders today.

The truth *can* be known, and we can live in accordance with it, even if it is sometimes difficult. What's more, Christians believe that truth is not just a concept but a *person*: Jesus Christ. To acknowledge him as true God and true man has led to many people's deaths up and down the centuries, starting with Jesus himself. Standing face-to-face with the Truth incarnate, Pontius Pilate condemned Christ to death with the quip, "What is truth?" (Jn 18:38).

By the way, in *Assassin's Creed Revelations*, I was finally given an explanation of that motto that satisfied me. As the protagonist, Ezio Auditore da Firenze, reflects on his life and his creed, he ponders, "To say that 'nothing is true' is to realize that the foundations of society are fragile and that we must be the shepherds of our civilization. To say that 'everything is permitted' is to understand that we are the architects of our actions and that we must live with their consequences, whether glorious or tragic." I put the controller down satisfactorily.

"Ah," I remember thinking, "now that I can agree with."

BEAUTY POINTS US UPWARD

"The sweetest thing in all my life has been the longing . . . to find the place where all the beauty came from," wrote C. S. Lewis in his work

Till We Have Faces.[4] We all must inevitably ask, dear reader, where does beauty come from?

The short answer is that beauty doesn't come from anywhere—it is simply one of the properties of being. Because a thing exists, it shares in beauty to some degree (some things more than others, of course). Ancient philosophers described the highest forms of beauty, truth, and goodness as "transcendental" (from the Latin *transcendere*: "to exceed") properties of all being. They argued that because we can judge things as being more or less true, good, and beautiful, we must have an innate sense of these transcendental properties.

If we see an act as good, for example, there must be something called the Good. How can I say something is true unless I stack it against the highest Truth? This beautiful creation of a sunset is but an echo of what must be Beauty itself. Plato and other philosophers thought that these transcendentals were real—more real than physical reality itself—and our life's goal should be to escape this realm of mere shadows to reach these eternal heights.

As a Christian, I acknowledge that God is the source of these highest forms of Truth, Goodness, and Beauty, and to the extent that we live consistent with them, we radiate God's being in this world. These transcendentals are thus the timeless and universal attributes of existence itself. We delight in these transcendentals, and they "speak" to us because we are meant to reach the unifying source behind them: God.

A person participates in all three of these transcendentals at the same time, like a dance that ebbs and flows, so there isn't a sharp distinction where beauty "ends" and truth "begins." They are more akin to a bowl of spaghetti, rather than three separate compartments that never touch. Priest and author Fr. Thomas Dubay notes, "Truth, beauty, and goodness have their being together. By truth we are put into touch with reality, which we find is good for us and beautiful to behold. In our knowing, loving, and delighting, the gift of reality appears to us as 'something infinitely and inexhaustively valuable and fascinating.'"[5]

"Beauty," wrote theologian Jacques Maritain, "is the radiance of all the transcendentals united."[6] Thus, when we experience something truly beautiful, we are also participating in some kind of goodness and so are standing before something that is ultimately true.

The transcendentals signal to us that there is something much more beyond ourselves. So that's why we experience the Beautiful as something objective—outside of just our own opinions and personal preferences—that stirs, captivates, and invites us to seek it out. When we seek, search, and scour the earth for the source of beauty, we will, in one way or another, arrive before the mystery of God. "Art demands an artist," wrote Fr. Dubay. "Random chance has never explained a waltz or a symphony, a physical equation or an epic poem. It cannot."[7] Priest and longtime preacher to the last few popes Fr. Raniero Cantalamessa writes, "To say that God is the author of beauty not only means that he created all the beautiful things in the world but that he also created the very sense of beauty, putting a love for it and a capacity to recognize it in the hearts of human beings, which we call the aesthetic sense. He wanted beauty . . . to be a ladder on which we ascend to him, the 'one who attracts,' the magnet."[8]

God is the "author of beauty" (Ws 13:3). Beauty is not an abstract reality floating around in the world of Plato's transcendent Forms; beauty is one of the fingerprints of the Divine Artist at work. "God created the world to show forth and communicate his glory," as the *Catechism* explains (319). "That his creatures should share in his truth, goodness, and beauty—this is the glory for which God created them." We are meant to delight in and participate in the beautiful things of this earth! This includes being "co-creators" with the Divine Artist and using our own gifts—be it in song, painting, writing, or game design—to create something beautiful with God for the world to enjoy.

WHOLENESS, HARMONY, AND RADIANCE

St. Thomas Aquinas, a priest and preeminent scholar of the thirteenth century, builds on this notion from the book of Wisdom to develop his thesis on the beautiful, stating that beauty occurs when three distinct elements meet: wholeness (*integras* in Latin), harmony (*consonantia*), and radiance (*claritas*). I promise that we won't get too lost in the weeds with the Latin here, so please hang with me.

By wholeness, or integrity, we mean the object possesses all qualities necessary to express its essence (a library filled with books makes it "whole"; a *Mario* game without Mario in it would lack something). Harmony, or consonance (think of the word *consistency*), means that the object is proportional and functions toward its proper end (a gym with a donut shop inside isn't consonant, while a military squad marching in unison presents harmony). Clarity is the object's ability to let its essential nature shine through clearly (a dirty windshield provides no clarity; a well-kept stained-glass window refracts the sun and reveals brilliant colors).

When all three of these facets align—wholeness, harmony, and radiance—beauty is manifested. Think of when an athlete has perfect form during the Olympics or when an orchestra has everyone playing in sync. A prime example is the medieval cathedrals, each of which is designed to represent these classical elements of beauty merged with breathtaking architecture. Healthy marriages and friendships can embody beauty as well, reflecting the wholeness, harmony, and radiance of true love.

And, of course, as we know, video games can be beautiful too. This is coupled with amazing graphics depicting sprawling landscapes and Oscar-worthy storylines detailing epic adventures. In short, gaming is the new place where beauty is being fostered and promoted in the entertainment industry.

JOURNEY: A CASE STUDY OF BEAUTY IN GAMES

One of the main reasons video games are the most popular form of entertainment today is their remarkable ability to manifest beauty. The best video games, while obviously fun to play, also offer thought-provoking stories filled with astonishing scenery and sweeping soundtracks. In short, a good video game fits Aquinas's definition of beauty to the letter—and whether we realize it or not, beautiful games put us in touch with our ache for God.

There are numerous examples one could give of beautiful games today. I love the dystopian, philosophically rich, beautifully designed games of the *BioShock* series. Several of my friends have loved *The Witcher* games or *The Legend of Zelda* series for their cast of unique characters and sprawling dynamic worlds. But let's shift out of the

AAA-game arena and focus on the work of a smaller company that produced an "indie" game that captured the hearts of everyone who has played it: *Journey*.

I had *Journey* for years on my PlayStation but never booted it up until one day (in preparation for this book actually) I invited my oldest daughter to play it with me. Having read enough reviews to give me faith that the game's content wouldn't give my kids nightmares and scar them for life, I invited all the kids to watch. They were all captivated.

Produced by thatgamecompany (TGC), *Journey* is a sheer work of art and throws many of the usual button-mashing mechanics out of the window. You are dropped into a stark desert with minimal instructions. A mountain is seen in the distance, so you start traversing toward it. There's no dialogue—*at all*—in the entire game. The story gradually unveils itself as you advance through the landscape toward the mountain and begin to make sense of everything. It's all backdropped by a gorgeous musical score by film composer Austin Wintory.

Yes, there are game mechanics at play in *Journey*—using the controller to move, for instance, or relying on environmental feedback—but this game showcases how modern video games can transcend mere mindless entertainment and become true works of art. Even though *Journey*'s production bankrupted TGC, it eventually reaped back its costs and then some, and went on to be nominated in eight categories in the 2013 British Academy Games Awards. CNN called it "mysterious and beautiful,"[9] and a writer at GamesRadar asserted that it was "one of the most amazing game experiences of my life."[10] Its soundtrack was nominated for a Grammy in the Best Score Soundtrack for Visual Media category. Mitch Lasky, a general partner of the venture capital firm that signed off on a five-and-a-half-million-dollar investment in TGC, noted, "*Journey* may be the video-game industry's 'Toy Story' moment."[11]

As I said, my children were all entranced by the game, and so was I. I let my daughter play the majority of the game, wanting to see it from her eyes. She was often caught without words to express her experience of the game, trying to decode the clues of the story while also being so moved by the beauty that she could only stare and wonder. From sliding down the sand dunes in an ancient city to escaping a subterranean maze and reaching the final summit of the mountain, *Journey* is an emotional, elemental masterpiece.

Games like *Journey* and so many others reveal several elements that harness beauty in video game culture. For our purposes, let us briefly focus on one of the most influential manifestations of beauty we experience in gaming: music.

THE POWER OF MUSIC

In 1985, Nintendo released its first major home-console game, *Super Mario Bros.* After the infamous "Video Game Crash of 1983" when most companies lost hope for the future of the gaming market, this game single-handedly revived the industry. Known for its exciting but simple gameplay, brilliant level design, and charming story, *Super Mario Bros.* garnered worldwide acclaim, solidifying a place in history both for Nintendo and their courageous plumber in his red hat and blue overalls. Yet, there was one more vital, even if overlooked, component to Mario's success: the soundtrack.

Up to this point in the gaming industry, music—and indeed beauty as a whole—was seen as something secondary to the mechanics of the game itself. If beeps and boops would suffice, why bother with anything more complicated than that? With *Super Mario Bros.*, however, the design team wanted to enhance the game with an iconic and complex musical accompaniment. They hired Koji Kondo to compose the now-legendary melodies associated with the Super Mario franchise. The success of Kondo's soundtrack made one thing clear: among the most influential components of a great video game is its musical score.

Since Kondo's watershed compositions, the gaming industry has made leaps and bounds regarding the beauty of music. Super Mario's eight-bit synthesized themes have given way to Emmy-award-winning orchestras playing masterful symphonies. In fact, there are a number of games whose music is just as popular as the gameplay itself. The pains of nostalgia run deep for many who hear "Ezio's Family" from Jesper Kyd's score for *Assassin's Creed*. Jeremy Soule's compositions in *Skyrim* can invoke a flurry of memories and deep emotions. For many of my peers, it was the *Halo* franchise that introduced them to Gregorian chant!

"Music gives wings to the mind, flight to the imagination, and life to everything." These words, attributed to the philosopher Plato, still prove true today, and you would be hard-pressed to find a gamer who disagrees. Music is not static like a painting or sculpture. Music happens in movement—from one bar to the next, and with notes that dip and move with breaths of silence in between—and we are invited into the middle of this dynamic dance. When we crank up the volume of our favorite song, it's because something inside us wants to *enter into* the music itself.

This participation in the art of music—whether as a listener or a player—mirrors the way we human beings exist. The human being is not simply a creature who just *is*—we are creatures "on the way," always in motion (whether we want to be or not) and headed toward an end. We cease to exist when we stop moving, just like music. To put it philosophically, humans are constantly *becoming*. We mature and grow, and no two days are the same. The human being is a pilgrim, a being who knows deep down that he or she is destined for more.

This ache for more accompanies every action and whim of our lives. Yet, it is among the most difficult reality to put into words. We cannot explain it nor dismiss the weight of existence. In every passing moment, as we observe the ins and outs of daily living, the question burns within us: *Why am I here?* and *What is it all for?* St. Paul called this the Spirit's "sighs too deep for words" (Rom 8:26); such promptings cannot be confined in the soul alone. It must be released in a shout, a yell . . . a song. And here is the universal power of music.

Some of the earliest historical accounts of a musical tradition are detailed in funeral rituals, so-called dirge songs, where the family of the deceased would wail in various minor tones trying to capture the devastation of death and share it with the community. Music is a language that makes known what words and deeds cannot. It captures the wordlessness of the soul. When we cannot speak, we sing.

Video game developers recognize the powerful role of music to the experience of the game. What began in the 1980s as the catchy background jingles of *Galaga* and *Tetris* have evolved into sweeping cinematic soundtracks of *Final Fantasy, Uncharted*, and *Skyrim*. Hollywood composers like Hans Zimmer, Harry Gregson-Williams, and Bear McCreary—artists whose talents were once reserved for multimillion-dollar international film blockbusters—are now turning their attention to video games and composing scores for the *Call of Duty, Metal Gear Solid*, and *God of War* franchises and more.

Video game compositions are spilling over into major recognizable awards as well. In 2011, Christopher Tin's track "Baba Yetu," featured in the video game *Civilization IV*, became the first gaming composition to receive a Grammy. "Colette," from Oculus Studios and Electronic Arts' Respawn Entertainment, won Best Documentary Short Subject in 2021, making it the first film from a video game to win an Oscar. More and more, the gaming industry is becoming the talent pool for our entertainment culture. The fact that game soundtracks are such a huge part of a game's development is clear evidence that gamers have high-browed expectations for the art they encounter—standards that exceed brainless stimulation. Video game soundtracks tap into our yearning for mission and community by blending the overall objectives of the game with whimsical and emotional musical themes that remain in our memories long after the final boss is vanquished.

THE WAY OF BEAUTY

Experiencing things such as the rose window of Notre-Dame Cathedral, a symphony of Beethoven, a stirring film like *Gladiator*, or the open world of *Zelda: Breath of the Wild* often leaves us without words and with a burning desire to enter into that beauty. In the case of a beautiful video game, it's easy to spend hours and hours playing because it's something indeed delightful and pleasing. When it comes to discerning the heroic life and finding meaning and purpose, beauty is an attractive signpost to begin exploring the bigger questions of life.

Pope Benedict XVI called this "Way of Beauty"—the *via pulchritudinis*—the most attractive route to God. Our generation, aimlessly atomized and fiercely individualistic, recoils at any command in what to believe or how to behave. Remember our discussion on truth and relativism? "You do you" is the slogan of our era. Any perceived judgment of another's lifestyle is instantly dismissed now as "hateful." But in placing what is beautiful before us, we are disarmed. "Hey, come look at this beautiful game!" we might say to a friend as we invite them to ponder it with us. *Why* is this thing beautiful? *Where* does that beauty come from?

The way of beauty is thus a helpful pathway to reopen conversations of depth and meaning, especially for our relativistic time today. It's a task we must take on seriously, though, for the consequences of accommodating ourselves to a world devoid of beauty, truth, and goodness are grave. Pope Benedict XVI warned that "when a culture attempts to suppress the dimension of ultimate mystery and to close the doors to transcendent truth, it inevitably becomes impoverished and falls prey, as the late Pope John Paul II so clearly saw, to reductionist and totalitarian readings of the human person and the nature of society."[12]

So while pursuing beauty is right and this way of beauty is a worthy means of witness, it must be mentioned that we can go off track whenever we mistake the creation for the Creator. The beautiful art, game, mountain, or person in front of us carries before our self-centered hearts the possibility of becoming an idol that we worship as if it were something that could fully satisfy our hearts. "Every man who knocks on the door of a brothel is looking for God," asserted English writer G. K. Chesterton. Misplaced worship is the agony of men and women up and down the centuries. Misery, dysfunction, and consternation are felt on all sides when we drink from wells that can never quench our ache for infinity. Bitterly returning as addicts again and again, we can corrupt the beautiful thing we once admired.

"Beauty is a terrible and awful thing," asserts one of Dostoyevsky's principal characters in the novel *The Brothers Karamazov*: "Beauty is mysterious as well as terrible. God and the devil are fighting there and the battlefield is the heart of man."[13] This is why the heart—the core, the center of the human person—and what we put at the center of our worship matters so much. "Blessed are the pure of heart," Christ asserts to his followers, "for they shall see God" (Mt 5:8). Whoever or whatever wins the heart, Jesus understands, wins the worship of the whole person.

Authentic Catholic Christianity is not the death of our desires but a *deepening* of rightly ordered desire.[14] We don't repress the ache for beauty in an unhealthy puritanism, nor do we indulge all urgings like an addict. Jesus calls us to live courageously, free of our false worship, so we can appreciate all the beauty of creation and participate in it joyfully.

We must affirm where we are finding beauty in our modern world—and in this book we are focusing on the worlds, beauty, and friendships that video games can offer—but also reorient our souls to point that ache for beauty toward God, who alone can satisfy. "You have made us for yourself, and our heart is restless until it rests in you," wrote St. Augustine in his *Confessions* more than 1,500 years ago. These words ring ever true for our hungry generation, and it is our task to continually lead others to the source of beauty that we all desire and where alone we find our rest.

BEAUTY WILL SAVE THE WORLD

The original ending of *Final Fantasy VII* lasts almost ten minutes, a cinematic feat for the thirty-two-bit games of 1997. After beating the final boss, players sit back and experience the catharsis of the story's characters coming together for the final push against the powers of evil. When all seems lost, the game ends just as it begins, with ephemeral strings, a moment of peace, and staring into the restful gaze of that beautiful girl.

"Beauty will save the world," Dostoyevsky affirmed in his 1869 work *The Idiot*. But what does that statement even mean? It sure sounds poetic, but is it correct?

Dostoyevsky largely leaves it up to us as the reader to grapple with its meaning, but as I understand it, if we follow the breadcrumbs of beauty in the world—in nature, soundtracks, games, friendship, love, architecture, and cathedrals—we will eventually trace it back to its source, which is ultimately *our* source: the Lord God almighty. In the face of brokenness and suffering in the world today, the beauty that we find in fragments seems to invite us back to where we can be made whole. That's how the flower girl on the dirty dystopian streets of *Final Fantasy VII* can serve as an invitation for each of us to pause, take in beauty, and be pierced to the very core.

QUESTIONS FOR REFLECTION

- How would you define beauty?

- What is the most beautiful movie, music, or video game you have ever experienced? What made it beautiful?

- Do you believe that God is connected to beauty? Why or why not?

6

HOW THE GAMES HAVE CHANGED (AND CHANGED US)

I remember playing the zombie horror game *Resident Evil 2* late at night in complete darkness on the original PlayStation back in the late nineties. "Let's play the scariest game ever with no lights on," my fourteen-year-old brain told me. I nearly punched my little brother in the face when he came silently shuffling up behind me, moaning like the undead. Years later, we would be shooting zombies together on one of the franchise's many sequels. The graphical updates, the creation of cinematic-level atmospheres, and frenzied collaborative action led to some heart-pounding and truly stressful sessions of bonding. The games had certainly changed in maturation, tone, and content.

I also realized how increasingly difficult it was to turn certain games off. Some of the role-playing games I played, such as *Final Fantasy*, required hours and hours of level grinding in order to beat certain bosses. I'm pretty sure that in one save file I logged in more than eighty hours of gameplay. I remember, too, one day in which my friend Victor and I played *Gears of War* for at least six hours straight—I sincerely don't remember if I went to the bathroom in that duration. All I know is that we started when the sun was out and when we emerged it was nighttime.

"I can turn this game off whenever I want to . . . right?"

I love games, and I have taken a largely affirmative stance toward them in this book. Games are indeed compatible with living a heroic life—but anything good can be overdone and abused. Because these gaming worlds are so immersive, we need to explore the "shadow side" of gameplay and examine certain pitfalls of the gaming scene today.

VIOLENCE?

When it comes to video games, a common fear is that gamers will not be able to discern reality from the virtual world—a fear that the boundary between the game and our lived life will be lost, leading to a life of isolation, despair, or even violence.

Despite media reports to the contrary, meta-analyses of video game research literature reveal no meaningful correlations between gaming and enacting violence in the real world.[1] This fear seems to stem from a holdout of the *Mortal Kombat* era of the 1990s when senators fearmongered in the U.S. Congress that games would corrupt an entire generation. (Fun fact: The original *Mortal Kombat* is the reason that the Entertainment Software Ratings Board exists and gives maturity ratings to games.[2])

We need to make an important distinction, though, between the presence of violence in a story versus a story that is advocating for, or glorifying, violence. Stories, movies, and games that feature violence for violence's sake can indeed be deformational to the person and his or her conscience, just as with the gratuitous display of sexually intimate acts. This is different than a story such as *The Lord of the Rings* that demonstrates the reality of evil in the world and our deep need to take a stand against it.

As Catholics, we have a deep confidence that God can be found anywhere. We delight in the goodness of rightly ordered beauty, nature, film, the sexual union between a husband and wife, and complex stories that tell us of redemption and the inevitable triumph of the good. We should prioritize prayer and discern our media, of course, but to be a complete and utter puritan would discount all kinds of beautiful art and modes of genuine leisure. To refuse to enjoy the company of "imperfect people" (ourselves included here, by the way), turn our nose up against an imperfect movie, or pass on an imperfect game is to miss out on the richness and complexity of human life.

Whenever we experience the tragedy of a school shooting, people wonder whether violent video games are to blame for motivating the shooter, but studies do not support that assumption. In nearly 90 percent of all school shootings between 1995 and 2003, the major factor was acute or chronic social rejection.[3] The authors of a 2019 study found that no tipping point was associated with the engagement of a violent video game and an increase in aggressive behavior.[4] Being outcasted and experiencing social humiliation can be experienced by a person both online or offline, and we know that the fallout from bullying—whether the recipient is eight or forty-eight—can be serious.

More than any violence in video games itself, it is the cocktail of isolation, humiliation, family abuse, and fatherlessness that often leads a person to enact any retaliatory violence in the real world. These are deep wounds that individuals carry, and we must become attentive to caring for them.

DEAR PRUDENCE

So while there is no conclusive study to show direct causation between playing violent games and enacting violence in real life, there is a formational question we must ask as Christians who bear God's grace and are called to holiness: *Should* I or my loved one be playing this particular game?

This question is about the virtue of prudence. And the honest answer might be, "*No*, the game isn't filling me up with good imagery or redeeming value. I ought to play something else." I've had to make this call a few times in my own life with movies, shows, and games. One particular series that I was enjoying had way too much sexual imagery inserted into every episode. It was gratuitous and disconnected from the storytelling. I realized that as much as I wanted to see how the story of the main character played out, it wasn't doing me or my marriage any good to continue watching this show.

VERBAL VIOLENCE

While there's no correlation between violence in video games and in real life, we're certainly all living through an era of unprecedented verbal violence toward one another, from all ages and walks of life.

We're all familiar with the potential awfulness of chat rooms and the comment section under any video or post. For now, at least, these cesspools come with the territory of online life. This is where the gift of technology can also be misused and even poisonous to ourselves and our human interactions.

One dynamic behind this dysfunction is the way anonymity functions—online, I am given the false sense that I am hidden and can say anything I want with immunity. The screen creates a buffer that somehow enables me to write and post things that I would never say to a person's face. This namelessness can bring out the worst in all of us and very clearly reveals our character (or lack thereof). The famous thought experiment of the "Ring of Gyges" was Plato's way of addressing this two thousand years ago: if you had a ring that could make you invisible (and enable you to get away with any behavior), what would you do? This reveals your *character*. Who are you when no one is watching?

Of course, there's also flaming, trolling, and the doxing of others. The last two decades of our immersive internet culture have fostered an atmosphere of polarization and echo chambers. If I post the "wrong thing" today (or even ten years ago), I could be fired, considered unhirable, or driven out of the virtual town by what we now call "cancel culture." In a time that has lost both a sense of Christian forgiveness and a general ability to forget (for what you tweet now lives on forever), it's no wonder that rates of general anxiety are through the roof in young people today.

ARE GAMES ADDICTIVE?

In August 2021, China enacted legislation that limited gamers under the age of eighteen to playing only between the hours of 8:00 p.m. and 9:00 p.m. on Fridays, Saturdays, and Sundays—for a total of three hours per week.[5] While a financially lucrative industry to its economy, China has had a complicated history with video games, having long suspected them as an ideologically corrupting "spiritual opium" import from Western powers. Beijing sought to curb video game use as early as 2000 when it banned gaming consoles. Chinese president Xi Jinping even called out the problem of addiction and personality shifts in the rising generation, blaming video games.[6]

Let's take a quick flyover of the recent data to see whether cur-rent video games can bring men and women to the brink of true "addiction."

While the debate is still ongoing in the medical community, increasing data suggest that video game addiction can be a real phenomenon. In 2018, the World Health Organization formally articulated this definition of "gaming disorder": "A pattern of per-sistent or recurrent gaming behavior, which may be online or offline, manifested by impaired control over gaming, increasing priority given to gaming to the extent that gaming takes precedence over other life interests and daily activities and continuation or escala-tion of gaming despite the occurrence of negative consequences."[7] Gaming disorder was recently considered a diagnosable psychiatric disorder, but researchers are still in debate because this is a new area of research and symptoms are not "one size fits all."

Anecdotally, many people can surely attest to the intensity of certain games and the visceral reactions a player can experience when they lose. Controllers or devices can be thrown, expletives can be yelled at the screen, and personalities can be seen to change for the worse the longer a person stays online without coming up for air. Games clearly are a way for us to channel aggression, but we must be aware and grow in self-mastery to make sure we're not losing control of ourselves in the process.

STUCK IN FLOW

The second chapter of Jane McGonigal's bestseller *Reality Is Broken* brilliantly lays out how gamers can easily attain the intense high that only the top athletic players can achieve—think of Tiger Woods, Michael Jordan, or Michael Phelps—in a fraction of the training time, and why it's a factor that makes it so hard for them to stop playing: "Video games took the traditional properties of potentially flow-inducing activities—a goal, objectives, increasing challenge, and voluntary participation—and then used a combination of direct physical input (the joystick), flexible difficulty adjustment (the com-puter algorithms), and instant visual feedback (the video graphics) to tighten the feedback loop of games dramatically. And this faster, tighter feedback loop allowed for more reliable hits of the emotional reward. . . . Each microlevel of difficulty you survived prompted a split-second emotional high."[8]

Whether it's *Tetris* or the manic chaos of an MMO battle royale, there's an addicting high when we improve with each round of play, as the game speeds up to increase the challenge level. This is why "just one more round" is never simply "one more round," and an hour of gameplay can easily turn into three or more. This desire in and of itself does not constitute a clinical addiction, but there are some developers with motives to indeed snare gamers with more and more dopamine-inducing mechanics that make it harder than ever to put down the controller.

DESIGNED TO HOOK YOU

Gaming companies are increasingly enlisting the help of behavioral psychologists, neurologists, and slot machine designers, using research and experience from the gambling industry to make their games as addictive as possible. Whereas a person once purchased a game and owned it for good (the cartridge, CD, or digital download), we now see the rise in endless patches, "seasons" of play, and "free-to-play" games. Free-to-play games, particularly on mobile devices, rely on the fact that a majority of players will play for free, but a minority will become addicted to the game and spend real-world money for bonus content (costumes, gems, upgrades, etc.).[9] Digital designer Golden Krishna notes that only tech companies and drug dealers describe their customers as "users" and that many features are added to "intentionally get you hooked."[10]

The younger a player is, the more likely they are to fall prey to these insidious tricks. Results of a 2011 study of 154 adolescents, all aged 14 years, leveraged MRI scans and found that frequent gamers had increased gray matter in the left ventral area of their brains, an effect similar to that present in the brains of gambling addicts.[11] Login "streaks," daily rewards, and randomized "loot boxes" also incentivize the constant desire for more, and some games even punish you for not playing the game—you don't want your crops on *FarmVille* to wither or your Tamagotchi to die, do you?

Some of the most tragic cases of gaming addiction are those that take their toll on marriages and families. In our digital age, many couples now meet online or even meet and start relationships (or even marriages) through the avenue of gaming, and I've met a few of them. Spouses who game together often report higher marital satisfaction, but there's also a danger in neglecting one's spouse in favor of the virtual.

Testimonies abound that detail the heartbreak many spouses feel if they become "gamer widows," spouses who feel abandoned because of their partner's inability to detach from their virtual play and prioritize the relationships and responsibilities to which they owe their due. A 2011 study observed that 15 percent of divorces cited video game addiction as the cause, which triggered many bloggers and cultural commentators to reevaluate our relationship with video games.[12]

"Addiction to drugs, alcohol, gambling, and social media have often been cited as reasons for relationship breakdowns but the dawn of the digital revolution has introduced new addictions," a spokesperson for the UK-based Divorce Online website claimed. "These now include online pornography and online gaming, so it is no surprise to us that more and more people are having relationship problems because of our digital addictions."[13]

Interestingly, many players themselves would admit that it's difficult to switch off from gameplay—"gamer's remorse" is a true phenomenon. Clive Thompson is a tech journalist for Wired, and after playing a dungeon crawler game for thirty-six hours in one week, he wrote, "The dirty secret of gamers is that we wrestle with this dilemma all the time. . . . The elation I feel when I finish a game is always slightly tinged with a worrisome sense of hollowness. Wouldn't I have been better off doing something that was difficult and challenging and productive?"[14] Every discerning player has to recognize where the hours of play are going and when it's time to step away to reconnect with the world around us and cultivate the skills and relationships in our lives.

USING TIME WISELY

Again, as followers of Christ, in all things we have to be discerning of the content we consume, how much we are intaking, and when we need to root out any disordered attachments from our lives. It's useful to ask ourselves, *What* are we worshipping?

I've had to restrain myself a few times over the years when it comes to the hours I put into games. Especially when I became a husband and a father, I had to realize that my family must get the *best* of my time, not my leftovers. My wife knows that gaming is good recreation time for me, but it doesn't come at the expense of spending quality time with my children. I've had to learn to set limits so I don't game the night away and be useless to my family the next day.

These kinds of decisions are easier said than done, but the sacrifice is always worth it. The game will be around later; the time with my children and the time I need to spend in prayer won't.

We must remember that every person and family must discern their limits, what content they can handle, and above all grow in self-mastery so that we can enjoy and master the things of the world without them holding mastery over us.

As we get ready to level up one more time, let's pause and remember that we must give our ultimate worship to God alone. When we're tempted to put any idol in the Lord's place, we must have the courage to either send it back to its proper station or pluck it out entirely (Mt 18:9).

QUESTIONS FOR REFLECTION

- What has been your experience of violence in video games?

- Have you ever been unable to stop playing a game? What were the elements that kept you plugged in? What trade-offs are you making with this use of your time?

- Where do you think the future is headed when it comes to games and entertainment? How do you hold on to what is true and good about gaming—what keeps you grounded?

LEVEL 3

7

REINTEGRATING OUR BODIES AND SOULS

I remember my first true virtual reality (VR) experience and how the whole living room was laughing at me. My wife and I were at a gathering with friends and someone who worked for a large gaming company brought a prototype VR headset for everyone to test out. The headset was connected to a TV screen so everyone in the room could witness what the player was seeing. Using two handheld joysticks, the player could move and interact within the virtual world.

There were only two games loaded in the system. One was a riff off of *Star Wars,* where the player could swing a laser sword in one hand to deflect enemy blasts and also retaliate fire with a blaster in the other. It was quite fun—like a full-immersion *Space Invaders.* But it was the second game that rattled me and still stays in my memory to this day.

The second demo was a simulation where you were taken up a very fast escalator to the top of the Empire State Building. The doors opened and, standing outside, you had to walk across a plank to step into Santa's sleigh. Now, intellectually I *knew* that this wasn't real, that I was in a living room and I couldn't die if I fell off that virtual roof. But in my body, it *felt* real. Everything in my body tensed up as my "fight or flight" response was kicking in. Eventually, my brain compelled my body to take a step—very light and gingerly—and I started putting one foot in front of the other. It didn't matter that I could hear a living room full of people laughing at me—my brain was screaming that I was going to die if this went wrong, darn it!

As I made it halfway across the bridge in the sky, Santa's sleigh within reach, someone from the party pushed me. Suddenly, now falling from the virtual roof, instinct kicked in: I tucked my knees in and began processing my impending death. Expecting to fall for a longer time, I abruptly hit the carpeted floor while the virtual world in front of my eyes continued plummeting. I pulled the headset from my face and stared at a room full of my friends who were unaware of the trauma I just experienced.

Heart rate still elevated, it would take me the rest of the evening to calm down and process what happened inside that headset. *I've been playing games forever*, I thought, *I knew that experience wasn't real . . . but it felt so real. My body experienced that as something real.* I still return to that mental memory from time to time and how that experience of VR unnerved me.

With technologies emerging with more powerful and more immersive VR devices, this capacity to "enter into" virtual worlds offers rich, new opportunities for gameplay and human connection. But we also risk losing something essential the farther we go down this rabbit hole of virtual reality: the necessary integration of body and soul that makes us human.

OUR EMBODIED EXISTENCE

Living the heroic life means living in accordance with reality—as we've examined already, this means being in tune with what is true, good, and beautiful. Let's take a brief detour away from gaming for a moment to ask this question: What does it mean to be an *embodied* human person? In other words, why should I care about the fleshy skin and bones that make me *me*?

To start, we are not solely spiritual beings. We are not angelic ghosts floating around, happening to inhabit a weird shell of flesh and waiting to ultimately escape upward. This is what the ancient philosophers like Plato believed though. I call it "Bugs Bunny theology," where the character dies from being crushed by an anvil, an angelic form floats away, and they're a pure spirit forever—but this is not authentic Catholic teaching.

We're also not simply animals—we aren't creatures driven only by instinct and mere pleasure. Some thinkers today try to assert we *are* just "more evolved" apes and claim we should make peace with the fact that our existence is only the result of atoms and neurons colliding together. It goes without saying that this would mean any attempt at living morally—naming something as good or evil, for instance—is a futile exercise.

Now we can *attempt* to live as either of these extremes—solely spiritual or solely material—but we inevitably end up frustrated because we were not designed as such. We were created as integrated beings, body and soul united together. Dr. Gregory Bottaro, a Catholic psychologist and author, writes, "Ultimately, our bodies are an integral manifestation of who we are as human beings. Our bodies are not something we *have*, but something we *are*. The popular sense is that the self is contained within the body, but the truth is we *are* our bodies. It is more accurate to say that our bodies are contained within us than to say we are contained within our bodies."[1]

Our culture is strangely fascinated and also totally dismissive of our bodies. On the one hand, we assume that we're simply "ghosts in a shell," mere collisions of brain waves and meaningless atoms, and our "real self" has nothing to do with our fleshy outer material; therefore, we can inject, amputate, and augment our bodies at will. And yet we also deeply identify *with* our bodies (rightfully so), and we want them to reflect our "truest self"—so again, we inject, amputate, and augment.

These dualistic philosophies run deep, and they have emerged in various forms throughout the centuries. We're most notably living under the shadow of the "Cartesian split," a philosophical principle in which René Descartes's dictum "I think therefore I am" made the individual person the sole standard of reality. Instead of conforming my subjective self to the objective world, I demand that the objective world (if one actually exists) conform to my subjective experience. This philosophical framework is the bedrock for constantly new and destabilizing trends of our modern times.

Our bodies and souls are seemingly at odds, but this is not the Catholic understanding of the human person! Philosopher Peter Kreeft writes, "Pre-Cartesian cultures did not divide reality into two mutually exclusive categories of purely immaterial spirit and purely nonspiritual matter. Rather, they saw all matter as in-formed, in-breathed by spirit."[2] St. Thomas Aquinas was in line with Aristotle when he described the soul as the form of the body.

We subtly acknowledge this truth in various ways; when someone strikes us, we say, "Why did you hit me?" instead of, "Why did you hit my body?" We're not angels—purely spiritual beings—and we're not mere animals who operate on instinct alone. We are this messy and beautiful composite of soul and body together. The simple truth is that we are our bodies and what we do to our bodies, we do to our souls.

SELF-MASTERY

"The hardest victory is over the self," Aristotle wrote. Remember the virtue of temperance that we named back in chapter 2? A temperate person is balanced in their pursuit of what's good and pleasurable— they have self-control and can master their instincts.

Self-control, even though it might require exercising that muscle of saying no and making limitations on good things, does not equal *repression*. Repression is the unhealthy refusal to look at or acknowledge legitimate desires and interior needs, such as our longing for connection, affirmation, or rest. Repressing our emotions only sweeps these needs under the rug, ensuring they will come back with a vengeance in a later manner and form.

Christianity is an embodied faith. Tertullian, one of the early thinkers of Christianity, asserted that "the flesh is the hinge of salvation." This is why the Incarnation (*carne* means "meat, flesh") and God's bodily existence on Earth is so important. Jesus's resurrected body foreshadows our own destiny to be raised to new life, body and soul! Death is now but a temporary stopgap in the narrative God is weaving. As Catholics recite in the Nicene Creed at every Mass, "I look forward to the resurrection of the dead," for in Christ, we hope in the renovation and restoration of our own bodies in the life to come.

It's of little surprise that nutrition and wellness coaches, programs, and resources have taken off in the last few decades. More people than ever realize how unhealthy, stressed, and out of sync we have become in regard to our bodies. Of course, the ache to also acknowledge our spiritual dimension must be addressed, and many nutritional and wellness programs adopt new age lingo to answer this need. Meditation is recommended, for instance, but never prayer, and some programs make an idol of wellness or dieting itself.

Back to gaming—when it comes to the hours spent online, we must remember the virtue of temperance and balance our digital play (and work) with time spent exercising, connecting with friends, enjoying hobbies and leisure, and praying. Fifteen minutes of silent prayer each day, either at a local church or in an outdoor space, is a great starting point to reorient ourselves to the God of the universe who is constantly knocking on the door of our hearts.

When it comes to the metaverse and the push to live in virtual reality, we should likewise approach these new landscapes with a discerning eye. Where might these platforms provide some good for humanity or even allow us to relate to each other and God in a new way? What are the dangers? How is this mode of existence reinforcing the further fragmentation of body and soul?

In the wake of the COVID-19 pandemic, many Catholic parishes began live-streaming Masses so that the community could still participate in Sunday worship. The problem is that it's easy to acclimate to having Mass on our own time, in our pajamas, with coffee in hand. The Mass is something incarnational that we must be physically present for; shoulder to shoulder with the Body of Christ, we receive the Eucharist, the very Body and Blood of Jesus himself. Watching Mass online is helpful for those far from a parish or currently sick, but we cannot receive the Body of Christ over a screen, and any attempt to live solely on the plane of virtual reality will always fall short of our God-given glory as human persons, body and soul composites.

We are called to honor and respect the body not as an end in itself but as a gift that God has given us so that we may love him and one another. We all have to face the doorway of death, and we shouldn't attach ourselves to any passing thing on this earth—even our health. We can enjoy the games and technology of our day, but we must remember to call ourselves and those around us back to the necessity of living in the physical world, being aware of our neighbors and those in need, and above all reintegrating ourselves to the reality of our embodied existence.

The Pixar movie *WALL-E* was strangely prophetic in its depiction of human beings becoming so comfortable in their mobile chairs with screens in their faces. They literally lost skeletal strength and became big babies dependent on machines for their existence. It was humorous during its release in 2008, but with the explosion of remote online work, two-day deliveries, and instant streaming, is it any wonder that we're feeling the results of these technological conveniences in our bodies?

Following Christ in today's culture—with all of the comforts and technologies and virtual realities never known by generations prior—means facing the challenge of living fully *in* our bodies.

ISOLATION AND REJECTION

The double-edged sword of prolific technology today is that while we are more connected than ever, our friendships are largely all mediated by a screen. The average millennial spends nearly six hours a day staring at a screen. Surprisingly, however, almost a quarter of millennials in the United States say they have no friends, and 30 percent report a constant sense of loneliness. Millennials have seen depression rise in their generation by nearly 50 percent.[3]

Millennials and Generation Z are the most technologically advanced and globally connected people in world history, yet they simultaneously suffer the highest rates of isolation. In the end, no amount of direct messages can fill the need for physical interaction. In fact, misuse of technology *stunts* the ability to relate with other human beings.

The increased usage of technology, especially smartphones, has led to a heightened sense of awkwardness and discomfort in social settings. Our young people want to have friends but are uncomfortable doing the one thing that is necessary to make them: turn off their devices and walk outside their front door. As a result, they seek means of camaraderie the only way they know how: through more technology.

As I've mentioned earlier in the book, games can allow us to carry the emotional weight of real-life relationships but without any of the risk. It's not a flesh-and-blood person making demands on us or our time but rather digital avatars—we can turn the game off whenever we feel done. The lack of real-world risk is part of the appeal of video games. In a game, I can "die" over and over again with no real-world consequences, or interact with townspeople and other avatars without the risk of rejection. Any trip to the airport, subway, or lunch table will reveal that we can all fall prey to spending more time with digital figures than making contact with the real people all around us. In the encounter with the virtual, we essentially enter a realm where we proclaim, "I make the rules. And you can never reject me."

This has profound consequences on expectations for human relationships, from friendship to dating and even parenting. To the extent that we operate within the rules of a video game, we have total control. This total control is something we can never exert over others, for the thoughts, feelings, and actions of someone else belong entirely to them. This is why, for instance, you can never *force* someone to love you. It is within the very nature of love that it is freely given, never forced. Once you attempt to coerce, force, or manipulate someone's love, it ceases to be love. Games do not pose this danger.

Neither does pornography. We are truly the "guinea pig" generation that is drowning in internet porn, with the average age of first exposure being twelve years old or younger.[4] A central facet to the allure of pornography is indeed that this fantasized reality will never reject you. Porn is like drinking salt water—it's a sad imitation that can never give relief to the deep ache we have to be seen, known, and loved. If you or a loved one struggle in overcoming pornography, I recommend checking out the website CovenantEyes.com or Exodus90.com to begin a journey toward healing, or reading *The Porn Myth* by Matt Fradd.

DEEPFAKING IT

With every new advance in technology, there are always unintended consequences. Technology is a tool, and we can use it rightly or wrongly. Game designers and companies continue to break through previously unscalable barriers, which leads to new opportunities for both good and ill.

Hollywood actor and director Jon Favreau (notable for his work on *Elf* and *Iron Man*) used a gaming engine to create the environments in *The Lion King* and *The Mandalorian* series. He also used what is being called *deepfake technology*, a process that allows a person in existing media to be replaced with someone else's likeness. With a deepfake, you can replicate a person's face or voice (living or dead) to simulate their likeness in video. Favreau noted that it's a double-edged sword that is exciting for storytelling but could be used for nefarious purposes. For instance, you could deepfake someone into security footage to frame them for a crime or place them in sexually explicit footage. The line between what we can determine as "real" and "unreal" will continue to become blurry in the future, as these technological advances are seemingly happening at lightspeed.

One of the most difficult things to re-create is the human face. From our times as infants, we are studying the faces of our parents—we read their eyes, the pores of their skin, and the subtle upturns or downturns of the lips as indications of mood. While the best computer-generated imagery takes us to new planets and offers us totally digital creatures (think of Gollum in *Lord of the Rings* or Thanos from Marvel's *The Avengers*), if something is "off" about the re-creation of the human face, it unsettles us and takes us out of enjoying the story. That being said, the sophistication of such technology will only continue to improve, and with it the need for counter-tech and some kind of ethical framework to function in a society where images of leaders and loved ones can be fabricated into positions of vulnerability.

BACK TO REALITY

One of the healthiest things we can do to regain a sense of balance in the digital world is to simply unplug and take time away to "reset" ourselves. Taking time in nature is vital for our well-being, from the health of our gut microbiome to our immune system and stress relief. Getting enough natural daylight into our eyes has been shown to help sleep patterns and our overall mood, and regular exercise does wonders for every part of our bodies.

Periods of silence and time away from technology are also help-ful for us to regain a sense of awareness of our bodies and the move-ments of the Holy Spirit. I have been blessed to take part in a few silent retreats in my life, where I spend time away from technology and distractions in order to be refreshed and experience the peace of God. These retreats have literally been silent—meaning no phone, no music, no games, and even no *talking* with the other retreatants. I usually go in with certain reservations, feeling the pain of detaching from my beloved devices, but always am reluctant to reenter the noise when the retreat comes to an end. I have done one-day, three-day, and also five-day silent retreats, and they are always powerful events.

As enticing as all our games and technology are, our human nature is meant to flourish in the real world. No matter how plugged in we are to our digital spaces, our full flourishing is found in the world around us—in right relationship with our families, friends, and fellow humans. Our bodies are a gift, and we *are* our bodies!

In striving for balance in all things and honoring our bodies, we will be slowly working toward living the heroic life and living as men and women of real integration who give glory to God in and through our bodies.

QUESTIONS FOR REFLECTION

- Do you feel "at home" in your body? Why or why not?

- What are small steps you could take to regain some self-control over your devices?

- What can you do to spend more time in nature and be attentive to your body?

8

IN THE SERVICE OF OTHERS

Many games have stirred me emotionally, with several bringing me to tears with their narratives and fully relatable characters. Some games have even pushed me to consider how my small actions in the world can directly affect others. *Red Dead Redemption 2* is just such a game.

Beyond the sheer beauty of its open world and Hollywood-level voice acting and performances, *Red Dead 2* is really an experience that moves us to consider our own finite time on this planet and our capacity to always return to the path of goodness. I've never loved Westerns or cowboy films, but *Red Dead 2* grabbed me with its almost tangible sense of nostalgia, the inevitable reality of death and our fight against it, and how our choices matter in the end.

Red Dead 2 invited me into a powerful story of friendship, the possibility of deep change, and (true to its title) the opportunity for *redemption*. The game revolves around the character of Arthur Morgan, a man living the outlaw life in the fading nineteenth-century American West. His gang is chased all over the country as their leader progressively becomes more violent and leads them down a path of destruction. Arthur is a gruff, disinterested Clint Eastwood type of character who doesn't care much for morality at the game's outset.

In one of the pivotal scenes of the game, Arthur is sitting next to a Catholic nun at a train station and tells her that he is dying, having contracted tuberculosis from beating a man to death earlier in the game. "I've lived a bad life, Sister," he says, coughing away. "We've all lived bad lives, Mr. Morgan," the nun responds, "we all sin." She affirms his inherent goodness, for she sees the internal conflict within Arthur—though he condemns himself, he's never happier than when he's lifting a helping hand to others. He still has time to do good in the time he has left.

Knowing that his death is imminent and admitting his own fear, Arthur is comforted by this kind woman's presence and humbly asks, "What am I gonna do now?"

"Be grateful that for the first time you see your life clearly," the nun replies. "Helping [others] makes you really happy. . . . Take a gamble that love exists and do a loving act."

"I shall try," Arthur affirms, as he escorts the nun onto the train.

TO BE A GIFT

No one is ever "too far gone," as we say in the Christian life: Peter denied Jesus, Thomas doubted the Resurrection, Paul persecuted early disciples, and Augustine lived a life of lust and vanity—yet we remember each as a saint. I have friends who fell deep into drug abuse and gang violence and who came back to a life of freedom in Christ and living soberly. I've made my own share of poor choices over the years, but God's always been waiting to welcome me home with his tender mercy and arms wide open, just like the father in the parable of the prodigal son (Lk 15:11–32). And if an uncaring loner like Arthur Morgan can choose to rewrite his story, why can't all of us?

Because we've been welcomed home and forgiven, we have a responsibility to others: to make amends, to give out of charity, to be examples of service, and to be a force of good for the world. Our culture is built around individualism, and it's easy to fall into the atomized, individualistic mindset where I'm only looking out for myself. This kind of narcissism is antithetical to the Christian life, a life that should be lived for the sake of building up others.

Today, it's all too easy to fall into a loop of self-centered actualization. We're told to never stop hustling and to always be improving ourselves: "Time is money, bro!" There are good elements within some of these messages, particularly when it comes to finding the motivation to fight inertia and better ourselves. But what's the point of our self-improvement in the end—what's the ultimate *telos* or goal of endless productivity and hustle culture? Is it just so I can reach my own personal Level 99? Or should my self-improvement go hand in hand with the need to walk with and help others along the way?

Remember, the heroic life is ultimately one that is lived *for others*. It's not enough to have leveled up every one of my real-world and virtual skills if it's only for the sake of my own glory. You can't take any of those achievements with you once you die! But we *can* use gaming and streaming for good—so let's look at some examples of how the online world has blessed the offline world.

GAMING TO HELP OTHERS

Streamers often rally support for charitable causes, local and large, and some organizations understand and value how gamers can use their competitions for fundraising efforts. For instance, Extra Life is a program of Children's Miracle Network Hospitals that raises money with a twenty-four-hour gaming event to support local hospitals that are part of the Children's Miracle Network. St. Jude's hospital system also has a fundraiser called PLAY LIVE that rallies players to raise money as they game and has raised more than forty-five million dollars for research and children struggling with cancer.[1]

Even outbreaks of war are receiving a response from the gaming community. Within the first week of Russia's military invasion of Ukraine in February 2022, several game developers pledged their financial support to citizens suffering from the war. *Destiny* producer Bungie tweeted, "Our hearts are with our friends and families affected by the events in Ukraine. We will be donating 100% of the proceeds of the first 48 hours of our Game2Give drive to humanitarian aid efforts in response to ongoing conflict."[2] CD PROJEKT RED, creators of *Cyberpunk 2077* and *The Witcher 3*, pledged to donate about $240,000 to the Polish humanitarian group Polska Akcja Humanitarna. Other developers also followed suit in an effort to not only raise awareness but also rally players to contribute in a meaningful way to help those most affected by the violence.

Games have also helped soldiers returning from active duty work out mental issues and find community. Research has shown how some games can help first responders deal with worst-case scenarios, help treat trauma in veterans, and help soldiers negotiate their own identity, particularly after returning to civilian life.[3]

Video gamers have even had a direct role in helping the Catholic Church. Notre-Dame Cathedral in France tragically caught fire in April 2019 and the roof was left badly damaged. The church is an iconic monument for the world, and the fire was deeply felt by both Catholics and non-Catholics. Support poured out from governments and institutions alike to help rebuild.

One of the key players in aiding the cathedral's restoration was Ubisoft, the developer behind the *Assassin's Creed* series. One of their games, *Assassin's Creed Unity*, was set in eighteenth-century France and featured a fully interactive Notre-Dame Cathedral that players could enter, climb, and leap from with abandon. "Level artist Miousse spent literally years fussing over the details of the building. She pored over photos to get the architecture just right, and worked with texture artists to make sure that each brick was as it should be."[4] Ubisoft pledged half a million euros to construction efforts, along with more than five thousand hours of this developer's research and 3D mapping of the cathedral, all with the hope that Notre-Dame would one day be restored to its original glory.

GAMIFICATION

The dynamic of gaming achievements is an attractive tool for audience engagement today, and we see it everywhere in the phenomena of "gamification." My good friend Google tells me that gamification is the "application of typical elements of game playing (e.g., point scoring, competition with others, rules of play) to other areas of activity." You've likely experienced it without realizing it.

Companies "gamify" products and services for us to become more excited to engage with them. For instance, apps can reward you with badges or bonuses for logging on subsequent days in a row. Snapchat used this feature, and I saw its addictive power in most of my students ("I can't hand in my phone for this retreat, Mr. Angel! It will break my Snapchat streak!"). Exercise counters, language apps, and even car insurance apps reward you for successive days logged in and offer daily challenges. The dopamine reward hit from gaming is real indeed!

These phenomena can snare us in time wasters but can also be used for good. The Bible app, for instance, rewards you with badges, daily motivation, and even planned seven-day "retreats" that you can tick off daily and participate in with a community of other members. Chastity apps like Exodus 90 and STRIVE help their members by gamifying their daily walk-in virtue and self-control, and can even alert friends when a moment of temptation strikes.

If we're made to game, we ought to tap into the power of competition and apply it to activities that help us grow!

STREAMING TO SHARE THE GOSPEL

Since the advent of streaming platforms like Discord and Twitch, gaming has exploded from only a means of connection with friends locally to an opportunity to engage with people all over the world. Obviously, as we examined earlier, there can be plenty of negative behaviors and vulgarities online, but we also find tremendous good. We cannot "throw out the baby with the bathwater"—we must use these avenues for good conversations and healthy witnesses to bring Christ to others.

For instance, Jonathan Blevins, who runs the Bearded Blevins handle on Twitch, games with a secular audience while consistently handling himself virtuously in the hopes of attracting others to the Gospel and the Catholic faith. While players might engage Jonathan for competition, they stay to chat, watch his streams, and even ask questions about faith:

> We aren't hosting teaching sessions and lecturing people. Faith comes up naturally after viewers have already begun to trust us because we are friendly and loving. Then when they inevitably ask questions about faith or life in general, they are very open to whatever we have to say. The number one comment we get from people is "Wow, I have never heard someone share faith in such a loving, non-confrontational way." . . . You don't have to talk about Jesus every second of every day to live out your faith. Everything we do can have God at the center if we are entering into it with the right disposition of our hearts.[5]

Jonathan is but one individual using video games to draw others toward God. I've seen priests and nuns streaming online, as well as many laypeople creatively using new apps and technology to "think outside the box" and bring the Gospel to new audiences around the world.

How might God be calling you to share the Gospel in a space or with people who need his Good News?

"I TRIED"

I could spill another book lauding *Red Dead Redemption 2*, but I'll rein it in here for one last reflection.

After Arthur confronts his gang leaders for their poor decisions and asserts that he's getting off the outlaw train because he's unable to follow their deceitful and murderous trail any longer, the gang turns on him—but not before the hand of the law, the Pinkertons, arrive. A chase and shootout ensue, and the player lives a final chapter with Arthur as he makes a definitive stance to fight for the good to his last breath. After spending at least fifty hours with the protagonist Arthur Morgan, I watched his stoic, uncaring character change into a man willing to lay down his own life so that a friend might live (Jn 15:13), a true gift of self.

"I *tried*," Arthur weakly utters, his near-last words of the game, as the sun rises on the character one last time.

At the end of the day, that's all any of us can hope to do: *try*. Do the hard thing. Take one step forward. Realize that this life is short and we're called to be a gift for others. Leave past mistakes behind. You are here in the present now, and it's never too late—for *anyone*. Do one little thing to make someone's life better.

Be a hero—make yourself a gift to others!

QUESTIONS FOR REFLECTION

- What do you think of when you hear the word *hero*?

- Have you witnessed games, channels, or streamers that help other people? If so, when and how?

- How have you experienced gamification in your own life? Where do you see it being used?

9

YOUR WITNESS AND MY WITNESS

"I just want to *do something* with my life . . ."

Tyler was a student of mine, one of the few juniors who actually paid attention in my class, and an overall amazing young man (I've changed his name here). He wanted to incorporate our course's teachings of morality and ethics into his life, but he was struggling. His usually joyful demeanor had suffered since his parents announced to him their impending divorce, and a hidden habit of pornography usage had returned full force—a coping mechanism to maintain some illusion of control and numb his pain, as he perceptively admitted to me one day.

Walking laps around the school's track, I listened to him share his heart, his concerns, and his fears. The teenage years bring a surge of hormones affecting the brain and body; it's also a time when we desire to "fit in" and yet also stand out in the world—usually without the means to take any concrete steps on our own. With so many forces beyond a young man or woman's control, it's easy to psychologically spiral and grasp for anything that offers a semblance of reliability.

Alongside the consistency of his water polo practices and our conversations about faith, Tyler found solace in the game *Stardew Valley*. Like *SimCity* or *Harvest Moon* (and all their sequels and off-shoots), *Stardew Valley*'s charm is in its simple operation: managing an inherited farm in which the player can grow crops, raise livestock, fish, forage, and socialize with virtual townspeople, all wrapped in retro-pixelated graphics with a lovely music score.

Tyler was not a "gamer," and he didn't care for his peers' obsession with *Madden, Fortnite*, or even *Call of Duty*. He didn't even play very often, but when stress levels rose at home and juggling all his responsibilities became too overwhelming, he gravitated to a farming simulation game to regain some peace and control. The problem was that he'd consistently play until 1:00 or 2:00 a.m., so on top of his family turmoil, his grades were also starting to suffer.

I kept walking with Tyler (literally and figuratively) over the next two years to listen and help him make sense of the circumstances of his life, share in the crosses he was carrying, and help him see that God did indeed have a plan and his invitation was always moving us toward a heroic life. Tyler just needed to keep taking one step at a time, control what little he could, and choose to trust in the plan of God, who was ever faithful to him.

MARTYRDOM

The theme of the previous chapter was service, calling to attention the fact that we are beings made for others, and so we can only become who we truly are, men and women of great souls (*magnanimity*), in giving to others. "It is better to give than to receive," the saying goes, because it's spiritually *true*. Look at Ebenezer Scrooge from Dickens's classic *A Christmas Carol*—in choosing joy, Scrooge can't help but be generous to everyone around him. We can find ourselves only by making a sincere gift of ourselves, as St. John Paul II affirmed.

It's easy to talk about being a gift—it's much harder to put this talk into action. But that's when our example shines through.

The word *martyr* comes from the ancient Greek legal term for "witness," someone who gives their testimony in a court of law. We've come to apply the term to anyone who "testifies" by their actions that they believe in their cause, particularly if they suffer for their convictions. Following in the example of Christ himself, Christians, since the earliest times, have been persecuted—from verbal abuse to death—for their belief in Jesus as the Lord. "If any man would come after me, let him deny himself and take up his cross daily and follow me," Jesus declared to his followers. "For whoever would save his life will lose it; and whoever loses his life for my sake, he will save it" (Lk 9:23, 24). To cling to life and security means you will isolate yourself, like Tolkien's character Gollum from *The Lord of the Rings*—a creature obsessed with protecting his One Ring, to the point where he becomes a literal skeletal version of himself. Only people willing to lay down their lives (Frodo and Sam, for instance, along with the martyrs of the Church throughout history) will consistently bear new fruit.

There are still martyrs all over the world. The twentieth century was one of the bloodiest periods in human history—more Christians died for their faith in this century than in all the other centuries of Church history combined.[1] In certain countries, believers must be cautious of displaying their faith in public and must worship underground lest they be jailed, tortured, or killed. If our necks aren't literally on the line, our reputation and popularity might be at stake should we choose to be a disciple of Christ. But this is the cost of love.

Putting our love into action will often look ordinary and humble—the sacrifice of our gift of self will likely take place in our own neighborhood, our dorm floor, our apartment complex, or our family. It can be as simple as a smile, donating a meal or old toys, or asking someone who might be lonely to game with you. What's important is to be inspired by the holy men and women who have gone before us—not to compare ourselves to them—and to ask God, "Whom can I serve with what little I have, today?"

THE BEAUTIFUL SAINTS

The Catholic Church is most beautiful not in the majestic cathedrals around the world but in her saints, the men and women like you and me who have chosen God above all things.

The Church contains saints known and unknown, who were teachers and preachers, nurses and scientists, priests, nuns, brothers, married couples, and single leaders. The marks of service and selflessness are found in the disfigured toes of Mother Teresa; the skeletal figure of Maximilian Kolbe, who gave himself up so a fellow prisoner could survive Auschwitz; or the imprisoned Cardinal van

Thuan celebrating Mass in the palm of his hand with a crumb of bread and a few drops of wine during his thirteen years of imprisonment by the Communist regime in Vietnam (nine years were in solitary confinement).

Everyone is called to be a saint, a concept we Catholics define as "the universal call to holiness." This is a profound insight informed by the writings of St. Paul as well as the early church fathers—each of us, from the moment of our baptism, is called to sainthood. This is a calling not just for priests and nuns but also for *all* of us as members of the Body of Christ.

That is no small matter! It is one thing to say everyone is called to be nice or be kind—it is a whole other thing to say we are called to be *saints*. Yet, that is what Christ himself asks of us. We are not here simply to "be good people." We are created not just to be nice but also to be *great* and to give our whole hearts to that call. The saint is the man or woman who, while never perfect, gets up again and again with every stumble, always offering the totality of their lives for the glory of God.

Saints come from all walks of life and every background imaginable . . . even gaming. Let's look at one saint in particular, a young man of our own generation who lived a life of integration—who loved video games, friendship, and the dynamic faith Christ called him to.

CARLO ACUTIS: GAMER AND SAINT

"To always be close to Jesus, that's my life plan," wrote Carlo Acutis, an Italian teen who died from leukemia at the age of fifteen, and the first millennial to be declared "blessed" by the Catholic Church (one step away from being recognized formally as a saint).

A young man of intense faith, Carlo grew up in Milan and enjoyed programming computers, spending time with his friends, and playing with his dogs. He felt an intense love for Jesus in the Eucharist from an early age and devoted four years to creating a website dedicated to documenting Eucharistic miracles around the world (the website is still viewable today!).[2] He also played games like *Halo*, *Super Mario*, and *Pokémon* with his friends.[3] He had a Pikachu stuffed animal that he hid from his dog on a daily basis. He was well loved by friends and talked with everyone, including the people everyone else ignored—the school janitor, cleaning crews, and the homeless.

Carlo put all secondary things in their proper place and gave all the first fruits of his energies to God. He attended Mass daily from a young age and had a deep devotion to the Eucharist and Mary, the Mother of God, praying the Rosary frequently. He served the homeless nightly and used his allowance to buy them sleeping bags and warm clothes. He also demonstrated amazing self-control, limiting his video game time on his PlayStation to one hour a *week*! (That's self-control that I don't even have!)

His mother, Antonia, who was never personally into her faith before the amazing witness of her son, noted that while most people Carlo's age lived "horizontally" (only concerned about life on earth), Carlo lived his life vertically, referring everything to God and eternal life in heaven.[4] She further noted that Carlo knew that gaming and the internet could be "an atomic bomb for good—but it could also be used for bad things which diminish the human person."[5] We need not be puritanical about the internet or video games, but, like Bl. Carlo, we are called to discern our media and how we can use it well.

During a sudden and painful battle with acute leukemia, Carlo said, "I offer all the suffering I will have to suffer for the Lord, for the pope, and the Church."[6] Three days after his diagnosis, Carlo died on the morning of October 12, 2006. During his funeral, which had a crowd that overflowed into the streets, people were already reporting miraculous events, claiming Carlo's intercession from heaven. Students, doormen, servants, and the homeless all came to honor him. His cause for canonization opened in 2013, and now Carlo is on the way to being recognized as a saint! Pope Francis even dedicated paragraphs about Carlo in his 2019 exhortation to young people *Christus Vivit* (*Christ Is Alive*):

> Carlo was well aware that the whole apparatus of communications, advertising, and social networking can be used to lull us, to make us addicted to consumerism and buying the latest thing on the market, obsessed with our free time, caught up in negativity. Yet he knew how to use the new communications technology to transmit the

Gospel, to communicate values and beauty. Carlo didn't fall into the trap. He saw that many young people, wanting to be different, really end up being like everyone else, running after whatever the powerful set before them with the mechanisms of consumerism and distraction. In this way they do not bring forth the gifts the Lord has given them; they do not offer the world those unique personal talents that God has given to each of them. As a result, Carlo said, "Everyone is born as an original, but many people end up dying as photocopies." Don't let that happen to you![7]

On a recent trip to Assisi, my wife and I were able to pray in front of Bl. Carlo's body where it now resides in the Church of Santa Maria Maggiore in Assisi. Sitting beside his casket, I couldn't help but think of our belief in the resurrection of the body—our belief that, after death and at the end of time, we will all be reunited with our bodies and receive the judgment given to us. We will see each other again, and others perhaps for the first time, and we pray to see God face-to-face. In Jesus Christ, who took on death and rose on the third day, we have been given the way forward, but we must all still pass through that door of death, the "Final Boss" of our game. How this will happen is a matter for God's understanding, not ours: "This 'how' exceeds our imagination and understanding; it is accessible only to faith" (CCC, 1000).

In that church in Assisi, I asked for Bl. Carlo's intercession over my family, that we might always put God first, and for all the readers of this book, that *you* might know how God sees and loves *you* and desires a life that is flourishing and radiant with the grace of Jesus Christ.

GIVE ALL GLORY TO GOD

As we look to envisioning ahead what God might have in store for our efforts in serving one another, let us not hesitate to think "outside the box" or dream bigger than we once did, for we are in new times that demand new strategies and tactics. How can you possibly use video games to spread goodness, truth, and beauty? How can you use your knowledge of web design, coding, or streaming to reach men and women of this generation to let them know that God loves them?

Remember Tyler, my student from the start of this chapter? He desperately wanted to "do something" with his life, something of worth. By the end of his senior year and certainly by his graduation, Tyler found himself on a much more solid foundation and was eager for the next chapters of his life. He ended up going to Notre Dame and found a great fraternity with other guys from the campus ministry, and even became a sacristan for his dorm's chapel. He's processing his parents' divorce with healthier coping mechanisms, including prayer and therapy. Now that he's graduated and in the working world, he leads friends and alums in informal scripture studies as he prepares himself for the married vocation. And he still plays *Stardew Valley*—but he tries to cut it off by midnight so he can get up in time for work.

Tyler is doing something meaningful with his life, and it is taking shape in small ways that are already blessing many other people and showing them the love of Christ.

In the end, God calls us to participate in the reality of the physical world and the realm of flesh-and-blood relationships, for that's where he meets us. We must encounter him in the realness of the concrete world. It is not enough for us to only defeat Bowser or win every round of *Fortnite*—that restless desire for more persists precisely because we were made for more, and we must meet these questions offline in the world around us.

Our humanity aches for real experience that involves our whole self—body, mind, and soul—and the most exciting thing of all is that we get to be the main characters in the real-life adventure awaiting us, where we can live a greater life than any virtual world can offer.

God is not in competition with us for our flourishing! To give ourselves over to Christ indeed means a painful surrender of all our idols, even good things—such as disordered attachments to health, career, fame, or video games—but this is so he can make all things new for his glory and for our own (Rv 21:5). We must be bold enough to go out onto the digital highways and "to the thoroughfares, and invite to the marriage feast as many as [we] find" (Mt 22:9). As I began this book quoting Pope Benedict XVI, allow me to close with a message of his from the very beginning of his pontificate, when he implored young men and women everywhere not to be afraid to allow Christ into the center of their lives: "And so, today, with great strength and great conviction, on the basis of long personal experience of life, I say to you, dear young people: Do not be afraid of Christ! He takes nothing away, and he gives you everything. When we give ourselves to him, we receive a hundred-fold in return. Yes, open, open wide the doors to Christ—and you will find true life."[8]

QUESTIONS FOR REFLECTION

- What does "being called to holiness" mean to you? What might it mean for you to follow that calling?

- What saints inspire you? Why? Whose story would you like to know better?

- Where do you think God is calling you to use your gifts and talents in the world?

EPILOGUE

"What now?" my brother asked.

We had just completed yet another entry of *The Legend of Zelda* franchise. Sitting through the end credits while reflecting on an emotional journey of adventure and exploration, we gave each other the same mischievous look.

I pressed Start, and with that, we began the story anew.

The journey always continues on!

A WONDERFUL ADVENTURE

The best games are the ones you can play over and over again, just like your favorite books and movies. You revisit the stories you love and you replay them with the people you love. There's always something new to experience. We will never have that final fullness of happiness we crave until the end of time, should we be granted to see God face-to-face in heaven. Until then, we are all pilgrims on a journey together—virtually and in reality.

Just like our favorite games, we revisit the stories of our faith again and again, year after year—not out of blind tradition but because they are *true* and are the most important facts of history: God called us into existence by love and for love, and has a plan for our lives. Sin entered the world, and we now experience a fallen human nature that is tempted toward selfishness and evil. But God sent his Son in the person of Jesus Christ almost two thousand years ago to take on our sin and redeem the world. Now we can walk in the power of his Holy Spirit, fed by the Eucharist and his Church, to go out and bring light into the darkness of our times, in worlds physical and virtual.

"Life with Christ is a wonderful adventure!" affirmed St. John Paul II, an avid skier, poet, philosopher, and priest who eventually was called to become the pope of the Catholic Church. He experienced a life filled with suffering—he lost both of his parents at an early age and watched his native Poland be overrun by Nazi and Communist forces—but he also experienced a life of great joy and purpose. He knew the paralyzing power of fear but also the love of God that is always present in the midst of suffering and uncertainty. "Take heart young people! Christ is calling you and the world awaits you!"[1]

The life before you may seem mundane and repetitive, scary and uncertain, or unexplored and thrilling. It's always a temptation to cling to safety and security, but these are not Christian virtues, and we will never know our greatness if we stay only in the safety of our harbor (physical or virtual). Ships were meant to hit the high seas. Likewise, we must be courageous and step out in faith, being bold in the one life we have been given.

Allow me to take a moment to recap our journey within this book.

We began by considering why we play games at all and why play is so important to our humanity.

We looked at how video games developed and why they've become such a force of industry and culture today.

We pondered what "the heroic life" entails—a life of virtue, pursuing excellence, and service to others—and how this call comes from being made in the image and likeness of a God who sees, knows, and loves us.

We located where the call to know your identity, your mission, and your community is embedded within the human heart and how these are echoed across many, many video games.

We examined how the true and especially the beautiful are echoed throughout games, as well as the good, and how important it is for us to be attuned to these transcendental realities to be fully human.

We've taken a serious look at some of the pitfalls that come from gaming today and living solely in the virtual world, affirming our bodily goodness and the need for integration and self-mastery.

And we've seen how it is in a life lived for others that we truly realize what we were created for—to become saintly men and women of the new millennium who can spread the Gospel online and offline.

Since every person is willed, that must also mean that they are willed *for something*. In the Church, we call this a "vocation." From the moment of our baptism, we are grafted onto the Body of Jesus Christ and are called to greatness. The heroic life is one in which we live well and serve others, in ways big or small. Whether you're single, married, celibate, a casual gamer, a serious gamer, or the parent of a gamer, you have a great mission and adventure before you.

Well? What are you waiting for?

Hit the Start button and get in the game!

ACKNOWLEDGMENTS

This book has been many years in the making, and it's here with the support of some great people along the way.

I want to thank the editing team and everyone at Ave Maria Press for believing in this work and helping to bring it to completion.

I am grateful for the witnesses of Bl. Carlo Acutis and Pope Benedict XVI, and for their intercession upon this project.

Thank you to Fr. Blake Britton for your friendship, support, and consistent tomfoolery.

Thank you to Nathan Van Coops for your encouragement and for always inspiring me to be a better writer.

Thank you to all my former students for allowing me to synthesize theology, culture, and video games. I hope that you maybe learned *something* from my class.

Thank you to my wife Jackie and our children for their love and for putting up with my long hours at the computer to finish this manuscript.

Thank you to my uncle Bob who lent my little brother and me his Super Nintendo decades ago—and to my parents who never made us give it back.

NOTES

INTRODUCTION

1. Benedict XVI, "Mass, Imposition of the Pallium and Conferral of the Fisherman's Ring for the Beginning of the Petrine Ministry of the Bishop of Rome," Vatican, April 24, 2005, https://www.vatican.va/content/benedict-xvi/en/homilies/2005/documents/hf_ben-xvi_hom_20050424_inizio-pontificato.html.

1. WHY WE LOVE GAMES

1. Teodora Dobrilova, "23+ Mobile Gaming Statistics Every Gamer Must Know in 2023," TechJury, last modified January 12, 2023, https://techjury.net/blog/mobile-gaming-statistics/#gref.

2. Catherine Lewis, "Video Games Were the Most Popular Form of Entertainment in 2022 by Far," Gaming Bible, last modified January 11, 2023, https://www.gamingbible.com/news/video-games-most-popular-form-home-entertainment-2022-740421-20230111.

3. C. S. Lewis, *The Four Loves* (New York: Mariner Books, 1988), 71.

4. Johan Huizinga, *Homo Ludens: A Study of the Play-Element in Culture* (Boston: Beacon Press, 1955), 2–4.

5. "Study: A Record 768 Million U.S. Vacation Days Went Unused in '18, Opportunity Cost in the Billions," U.S. Travel Association, last modified August 16, 2019, https://www.ustravel.org/press/study-record-768-million-us-vacation-days-went-unused-18-opportunity-cost-billions.

6. Jane McGonigal, *Reality Is Broken: Why Games Make Us Better and How They Can Change the World* (New York: Penguin, 2011), 21.

7. McGonigal, *Reality Is Broken*, 21.

8. Bernard Suits, *The Grasshopper: Games, Life, and Utopia* (Ontario: Broadview Press, 2005), 38.

2. WHAT IS THE GOOD LIFE?

1. PlayStation New Zealand, "PlayStation | Greatness Awaits," YouTube, June 19, 2013, https://www.youtube.com/watch?v=_B8PK-eg2QY.

2. C. S. Lewis, *The Weight of Glory and Other Addresses* (New York: HarperCollins, 2001), 26.

3. Fulton J. Sheen, *Ways to Inner Peace* (Mansfield Centre, CT: Martino Publishing, 2016), 33.

4. Jason Craig, "Made for Greatness?," Those Catholic Men, last modified January 17, 2017, https://thosecatholicmen.com/articles/made-for-greatness.

5. Charles Murphy, "The Good Life from a Catholic Perspective: The Challenge of Consumption," United States Conference of Catholic Bishops, last modified 2014, https://www.usccb.org/resources/good-life-catholic-perspective-challenge-consumption.

6. Edward Sri, *The Art of Living: The Cardinal Virtues and the Freedom to Love* (San Francisco: Ignatius Press, 2021), 2.

7. Alexander Kriss, *The Gaming Mind: A New Psychology of Videogames and the Power of Play* (New York: The Experiment, 2020), 188.

3. WHAT DOES GAMING HAVE TO DO WITH GOD?

1. Catholic Church, *The Divine Office*, vol. 1 (London: Collins, 1974), 67.

2. Damian Ference, *The Strangeness of Truth: Vibrant Faith in a Dark World* (Boston: Pauline Books & Media, 2019), 3.

3. James Schall, *The Order of Things* (San Francisco: Ignatius Press, 2007), 22.

4. Ministère de la Culture, "Lascaux," accessed January 31, 2023, https://archeologie.culture.gouv.fr/lascaux/en.

5. G. K. Chesterton, *Orthodoxy* (London: Willian Clowes and Sons, 1934), 134.

6. David Sheff, *Game Over: How Nintendo Conquered the World* (Wilton, CT: GamePress, 1999), 51.

7. Richard Stanton, *A Brief History of Video Games* (Philadelphia: Running Press, 2015), 124.

4. IDENTITY, MISSION, AND COMMUNITY

1. Debbie Lord, "Michael Phelps Says He Considered Taking His Life; Credits 'Purpose Driven Life' for Helping Him," Boston 25 News, last modified August 12, 2016, https://www.boston25news.com/news/trending-now/michael-phelps-says-he-considered-taking-his-life-credits-purpose-driven-life-for-helping-him/421312714.

2. "Michael Phelps Raising Mental Health Awareness after His Own Battle," ESPN, accessed January 31, 2023, https://www.espn.com/video/clip/_/id/29190338.

3. *Secrets of a Soul: Padre Pio's Letters to His Spiritual Directors*, ed. Gianluigi Pasquale, trans. Elvira G. DiFabio (Boston: Pauline Books & Media, 2002), 121.

4. Markham Heid, "Depression and Suicide Rates Are Rising Sharply in Young Americans, New Report Says. This May Be One Reason Why," *Time*, March 14, 2019, https://time.com/5550803/depression-suicide-rates-youth.

Notes 101

5. *Seneca: Selected Philosophical Letters*, trans. Brad Inwood (Oxford: Oxford University Press, 2007), 51.

6. Edward Castranova, *Life Is a Game: What Game Design Says About the Human Condition* (New York: Bloomsbury Academic, 2021), x.

7. Castranova, *Life Is a Game*, 8.

8. McGonigal, *Reality Is Broken*, 101.

9. Viktor E. Frankl, *Man's Search for Meaning* (Boston: Beacon Press, 2006), 109.

10. George Vaillant, "Yes, I Stand by My Words, 'Happiness Equals Love—Full Stop,'" *Positive Psychology News*, July 16, 2009, https://positivepsychologynews.com/news/george-vaillant/200907163163.

11. Colin Campbell, "Why Is Fortnite Battle Royale So Wildly Popular?" Polygon, March 30, 2018, https://www.polygon.com/fortnite-battle-royale/2018/3/30/17177068/why-is-fortnite-popular.

12. Brian Feldman, "The Most Important Video Game on the Planet: How *Fortnite* Became the Instagram of Gaming," *New York Magazine Intelligencer*, last modified July 2018, https://nymag.com/intelligencer/2018/07/how-fortnite-became-the-most-popular-video-game-on-earth.html.

13. Robert Putnam, *Bowling Alone: The Collapse and Revival of American Community* (New York: Simon & Schuster, 2020), 422–23.

14. "Teenager Having Seizure Saved by Online Gamer—5,000 Miles Away in Texas," BBC News, January 10, 2020, https://www.bbc.com/news/uk-england-merseyside-51063009.

15. Stanton, *Brief History*, 247.

5. THE BEAUTIFUL BECKONS

1. Augustine, *Confessions,* ed. Henry Chadwick (Oxford: Oxford University Press, 1998), 230.

2. Hermann Rauschning, *The Voice of Destruction* (New York: G. P. Putnam's Sons, 1940), 223.

3. Quoted in Chris Stefanick, *Absolute Relativism: The New Dictatorship and What to Do About It* (San Diego: Catholic Answers, 2011), 21.

4. C. S. Lewis, *Till We Have Faces: A Myth Retold* (New York: First Mariner Books, 1980), 75.

5. Thomas Dubay, *The Evidential Power of Beauty: Science and Theology Meet* (San Francisco: Ignatius Press, 1999), 23.

6. Jacques Maritain, *Creative Intuition in Art and Poetry* (Princeton: Princeton University Press, 1953), 162.

7. Dubay, *Evidential Power of Beauty*, 65.

8. Raniero Cantalamessa, *Contemplating the Trinity: The Path to the Abundant Christian Life*, trans. Marsha Daigle-Williamson (Ijamsville, MD: The Word Among Us Press, 2007), 75.

9. "'Journey' and the Rewards of Contemplative Gaming," CNN, March 9, 2012, https://www.cnn.com/2012/03/09/living/journey-and-the-rewards-of-con-templative-gaming/index.html.

10. Tom Magrino, "Why Journey Is One of the Greatest Games Ever Made," GamesRadar, December 12, 2012, https://www.gamesradar.com/why-journey-one-greatest-games-ever-made/.

11. Laura Parker, "A Journey to Make Video Games into Art," *New Yorker*, August 2, 2013, https://www.newyorker.com/tech/annals-of-technology/a-journey-to-make-video-games-into-art.

12. Benedict XVI, "Address of His Holiness Benedict XVI to the Bishops of the United States of America on Their 'Ad Limina' Visit," Holy See, January 19, 2012, https://www.vatican.va/content/benedict-xvi/en/speeches/2012/january/documents/hf_ben-xvi_spe_20120119_bishops-usa.html.

13. Fyodor Dostoyevsky, *The Brothers Karamazov* (New York: Dover, 2005), 94.

14. Christopher West, *Fill These Hearts: God, Sex, and the Universal Longing* (New York: Image, 2012), 18.

6. HOW THE GAMES HAVE CHANGED (AND CHANGED US)

1. Andrew K. Przybylski, "Scholars' Open Statement to the APA Task Force on Violent Media," September 26, 2013, http://www.christopherjferguson.com/APA%20Task%20Force%20Comment1.pdf.

2. Phill Alexander, *Esports for Dummies* (Indianapolis: Wiley, 2020), 97.

3. Craig A. Anderson and Wayne A. Warburton, "The Impact of Violent Video Games: An Overview," in *Growing Up Fast and Furious: Reviewing the Impacts of Violent and Sexualized Media on Children*, ed. W. Warburton and D. Braunstein, (Annandale, NSW: The Federation Press, 2012), 56–84, https://www.researchgate.net/profile/Craig-Anderson-19/publication/260487613_The_impact_of_violent_video_games_An_overview/links/580e823b08ae47535247b63d/The-impact-of-violent-video-games-An-overview.pdf.

4. Rashmi Parmar and Julian Lagoy, "Is Video Game Addiction a Disorder?," *Psychiatric Times* 38, no. 10 (October 4, 2021), https://www.psychiatrictimes.com/view/is-video-game-addiction-a-disorder.

5. Matt Haldane, "China vs Video Games: Why Beijing Stopped Short of a Gaming Ban, Keeping Tencent and NetEase Growing amid Crackdown," *South China Morning Post*, November 19, 2021, https://www.scmp.com/tech/big-tech/article/3156540/china-vs-video-games-why-beijing-stopped-short-gaming-ban-keeping.

6. Chris Buckley, "China Tightens Limits for Young Online Gamers and Bans School Night Play," *New York Times*, October 1, 2021, https://www.nytimes.com/2021/08/30/business/media/china-online-games.html.

7. "Addictive Behaviours: Gaming Disorder," World Health Organization, October 22, 2020, https://www.who.int/news-room/questions-and-answers/item/addictive-behaviours-gaming-disorder.

8. McGonigal, *Reality Is Broken*, 41.

9. Joshua Krook, "The Business of Addiction: How the Video Gaming Industry Is Evolving to Be Like the Casino Industry," The Conversation, September 12, 2017, https://theconversation.com/the-business-of-addiction-how-the-video-gaming-industry-is-evolving-to-be-like-the-casino-industry-83361.

10. Manoush Zomorodi, *Bored and Brilliant: How Spacing Out Can Unlock Your Most Productive and Creative Self* (New York: St. Martin's Press, 2017), 87.

11. Simone Kühn et al., "The Neural Basis of Video Gaming," *Translational Psychiatry* 1, no. 11 (2011): 53, https://doi.org/10.1038/tp.2011.53.

12. "How Video Games Impact Marriage and Divorce," Goldberg Jones, July 12, 2022, https://www.goldbergjones-sandiego.com/divorce/video-games-impact-divorce.

13. Matt Keenan, "Is Fortnite Becoming a Relationship Wrecker?" Divorce Online, September 7, 2018, https://www.divorce-online.co.uk/blog/is-fortnite-becoming-a-relationship-wrecker.

14. Clive Thompson, "Battle with 'Gamer Regret' Never Ceases," Wired, September 10, 2007, https://www.wired.com/2007/09/battle-with-gamer-regret-never-ceases.

7. REINTEGRATING OUR BODIES AND SOULS

1. Gregory Bottaro, *The Mindful Catholic: Finding God One Moment at a Time* (North Palm Beach, FL: Wellspring, 2018), 49.

2. Peter Kreeft, *Everything You Wanted to Know About Heaven* (San Francisco: Ignatius Press, 1990), 86.

3. Hillary Hoffower and Allana Akhtar, "Lonely, Burned Out, and Depressed: The State of Millennials' Mental Health in 2020," *Insider*, last modified October 10, 2020, https://www.businessinsider.com/millennials-mental-health-burnout-lonely-depressed-money-stress.

4. "Pornography Statistics," Covenant Eyes, accessed January 31, 2023, https://www.covenanteyes.com/pornstats.

8. IN THE SERVICE OF OTHERS

1. St. Jude PLAY LIVE, accessed January 31, 2023, https://www.stjude.org/get-involved/other-ways/video-game-charity-event.html.

2. Bungie (@Bungie), "Our hearts are with our friends and families affected by the events in Ukraine," Twitter, February 24, 2022, 7:03 p.m., https://twitter.com/bungie/status/1496999197559693321?lang=en.

3. West Virginia University, Eberly College of Arts and Sciences, "Video Games Offer Active Military, Veterans Coping Mechanism for Stress," ScienceDaily, June 22, 2017, https://www.sciencedaily.com/releases/2017/06/170622122756.htm.

4. Lara Jackson, "Assassin's Creed: Unity Will Be Used to Help Rebuild Notre Dame," GameByte, April 16, 2019, https://www.gamebyte.com/assassins-creed-unity-will-be-used-to-help-rebuild-notre-dame.

5. J-P Mauro, "Catholic Gamer Talks Evangelism on Twitch Streams," Aleteia, May 26, 2022, https://aleteia.org/2022/05/26/catholic-gamer-talks-evangelism-on-twitch-streams.

9. YOUR WITNESS AND MY WITNESS

1. Dan Wooding, "Modern Persecution," Christianity.com, May 3, 2010, https://www.christianity.com/church/church-history/timeline/1901-2000/modern-persecution-11630665.html.

2. Carlo Acutis, "Miracles List: The Eucharistic Miracles of the World," accessed January 31, 2023, http://www.miracolieucaristici.org/en/Liste/list.html.

3. Courtney Mares, "Beatification of Carlo Acutis: The First Millennial to Be Declared Blessed," Catholic News Agency, October 10, 2020, https://www.catholicnewsagency.com/news/46167/beatification-of-carlo-acutis-the-first-millennial-to-be-declared-blessed.

4. Sabrina Arena Ferrisi, *Blessed Carlo Acutis: The Amazing Discovery of a Teenager in Heaven* (Cramerton, NC: Holy Heroes, 2022), 33.

5. Ferrisi, *Blessed Carlo Acutis*, 37.

6. Ferrisi, *Blessed Carlo Acutis*, 67.

7. Francis, "*Christus Vivit*: Post-Synodal Exhortation to Young People and to the Entire People of God," Holy See, March 25, 2019, https://www.vatican.va/content/francesco/en/apost_exhortations/documents/papa-francesco_esortazione-ap_20190325_christus-vivit.html.

8. Benedict XVI, "Mass, Imposition of the Pallium."

EPILOGUE

1. John Paul II, *The Meaning of Vocation* (Princeton: Scepter, 1997), 23.

Bobby Angel is a Catholic author, speaker, and mentor-in-training with the CatholicPsych Institute with more than twenty years of experience in ministry. He is the coauthor with his wife, Jackie, of *Pray, Decide, & Don't Worry* (also with Fr. Mike Schmitz) and *Forever: A Catholic Devotional for Your Marriage*. Angel contributed to the books *Catholicism after Coronavirus*, *Wisdom and Wonder*, and *The New Apologetics*.

He earned bachelor's degrees from the University of Florida and St. John Vianney College Seminary and master's degrees from the St. Vincent DePaul Regional Seminary and the Augustine Institute. He trained at the Theology of the Body Institute. He also worked as a certified firefighter and emergency medical technician.

Angel has spoken at NCYC, the Good News Conference, Life Teen retreats, and diocesan youth conferences. He is a regular on Bearded Blevins's *Around the Halo* on Twitch, on the *Ascension Presents* YouTube channel, and the *God and Gaming* video series with Fr. Blake Britton. He contributes to the *National Catholic Register* and served as a fellow of parish life at the Word on Fire Institute.

He lives with his family in the Dallas, Texas, area.

Jackieandbobby.com
Instagram: @bobby.angel
YouTube: https://www.youtube.com/@jackieandbobby

Jonathan "Bearded" Blevins is the founder of BeardedBlevins Stream Team and Little Flower Media.

AVE
AVE MARIA PRESS

Founded in 1865, Ave Maria Press,
a ministry of the Congregation of
Holy Cross, is a Catholic publishing
company that serves the spiritual and
formative needs of the Church and its
schools, institutions, and ministers;
Christian individuals and families; and
others seeking spiritual nourishment.

For a complete listing of titles from

Ave Maria Press

Sorin Books

Forest of Peace

Christian Classics

visit www.avemariapress.com

AVE MARIA PRESS
Notre Dame, IN
A Ministry of the United States Province of Holy Cross